Mary & Fr
Thanks f
God
Peter Karanja

REVEALED

PATHWAY to GREATNESS

11 Keys to Unlock Your Potential and Usher You to Your Greatest Level of Success

Peter Karanja

REVEALED

PATHWAY
to
GREATNESS

Library of Congress Control Number 2013909365
ISBN: 9780989479103

International Christian Leadership Press
Saint Louis, Missouri

ꕥ

ACKNOWLEDGEMENT

This book would not have been possible without the support and encouragement of my wife, Damaris Karanja. Words cannot express my gratitude for your critique, ideas, proofreading and assistance in editing and polishing this manuscript. For understanding my long nights at the computer, I'd like to thank my two girls, Isabella and Olivia.

Special thanks to Randy Rohler for the long days spent typesetting this book and for the cover design; to Brentwood Publishers Group, thank you for making this dream come true.

ജ്ഞ

TABLE OF CONTENTS

ﷺ

CHAPTER 1

Introduction

"When courage, persistence, faith, and action meet, they wipe out the fear that holds us back from achieving our greatest level of success."

~ Karlene Sinclair-Robinson ~

Each one of us aspires to live a successful life, but often success seems elusive to a great majority. The fact is that success is not reserved for a chosen few. God has already promised you a life of abundance.

You are made in God's own image and likeness and therefore have an inborn ability to plan and be great. *REVEALED - PATHWAY to GREATNESS;* walks you through an eleven step process that will help you discover and unlock the potential within you and help wipe out the fear that holds you back from achieving your greatest level of success.

In the current fast-paced world, juggling tasks at home, workplace, at social events, and places of worship can be daunting. You often find yourself overwhelmed trying to accomplish multiple tasks with too little time and resources. At the end, you are baffled by the dismal outcomes or what King Solomon would have referred to as *'chasing the wind'*.[1]

As we navigate through the stormy and rocky terrain towards becoming what God wants us to be, we need to employ various strategies that align our ambitions with God's purpose over our life.

The synergistic alignment between you and God leads to a perfect shift of your ambitions to God's plans

The good news is that the seed of success is already in you. Deep within you there is untapped potential that is tagged to a God-controlled rudder that can steer you to your destiny.

You can unleash this potential by seeking God's guidance which leads to a divine connection between your mind and God's mind, your spirit and God's Spirit, your heart and God's heart, your will and God's will, your desires and God's desires, during which there is a download of revelations from God's Spirit into your spirit.

The synergistic alignment between you and God leads to a perfect shift of your ambitions to God's plans resulting in a God-centered vision. This realignment, coupled with proper planning sets in motion a series of open doors that will usher you to your divine destiny. The realignment also triggers your God-centered vision to be in harmony with your family, your values, your God-given ministry or area of service, and with your social and professional circles. This helps prevent any conflict between your vision and these areas. A conflict could potentially derail or stall your progress which may be costly to restore.

Attaining a God-centered vision calls for a change or a shift in your mindset that often seems to be very scary. Frequently you will notice that as soon as you change your mindset and decide to take that positive action, your mind is inundated with boggling questions. You wonder if your vision will really work or what will happen if you fail or succeed.

This book will help you navigate through the process of successfully establishing, aligning and implementing a God-centered vision. It will help you to remain focused on your vision and defy the popular approach of achieving an outcome by employing your creative ideas to achieve a popular outcome.

Envision Your Vision

REVEALED - PATHWAY to GREATNESS; will help you identify diverse ways through which God can reveal His plan over your life. Whichever way He chooses to confirm His purpose over your life; purpose to envision your vision with the end in mind. Plan to picture the path and the final outcome as God reveals it to you way before any noticeable activity takes place.

This can be achieved by taking the first concrete step

to develop what I refer to as *the Habakkuk Plan*. I will walk you through the process of developing *the Habakkuk Plan* after which you will be in a position to clearly understand the plan and your obligations as the vision carrier.

At one point or another, you've probably lit a lamp and hopefully placed it on lamp stand rather than under a bowl. In the same manner we will see how you can illuminate that God-given vision and keep it shining to the world. Remember, you are the salt and the light of the world, and your vision may be just what the world needs to see.

Just like a bridle is used to direct a fast moving horse to victory at the derby, prepare to use your simple but powerful vision as a guide to propel your dreams to greater heights. Developing a vision is very important. Do not neglect having one as this is the first step towards achieving your greatest level of success.

Strategize Your Vision

Your vision more often than not will define who you are, as well as who you are about to become. Carefully use it to map out your goals and action plan. This can be achieved by defining your goals prior to implementation; discovering what the Lord has already put in your hands, and seizing any available opportunities. I will walk you through the process of identifying your strengths as well as limitations or the blunt areas of your life that need to be sharpened.

You will also learn the importance of breaking down your vision into small manageable tasks and the process of prioritizing your short term or long term goals appropriately.

Prioritization of goals and tasks can be achieved

using three unique approaches discussed in this book namely; *the MAP approach, the GPS approach,* and *the Bull's eye Task Matrix approach*. These approaches will help you determine the urgency, importance and relevance of your goals in relation to your vision.

Pressing-on Towards the Mark

You have probably found yourself making New Year resolutions hoping to see change at the end of twelve months, only to lose passion and interest in twelve days. You give up prematurely either due to frustrations or due to unforeseen events that may stem from improper planning. When you build the foundation of your vision on Godly principles and engage in proper planning; you will notice that with determination, all things are possible through Christ who strengthens you.

Do not discount starting with those baby steps; they are worth than taking no step at all. The steps may seem small but they will one day be giant strides that propel you towards your providence. Watch out! Do not to be a captive of past failures or an attitude of 'I cannot do it'. Rather be liberated by the truth that 'you can do all things through the strength of Christ'.

Blessed to be a Blessing

Achieving your personal goals is only one aspect of realizing your destiny. It is God's intention that we reach out to those who are in need and share their burdens. By helping others, you are not only a blessing to them but you reap a blessing too.

The scriptures say that blessed is the hand that gives than the one that receives; this hand that gives will be blessed. Have you ever noted that the scripture says 'the hand that gives' but not 'the believer that gives'? Giving triggers blessings regardless of who the giver is.

There are many avenues that the Lord has opened for us to be a blessing. Whether it is giving at your house of worship; visiting that needy person, or giving to your local community, it is never in vain. Plough back.

Seek ye First

More often than not, we seek God's guidance as we prepare to start a project or when we face challenges, but fail to do so when we hit a home-run.

As you will see in this book, an honest prayer 'seals the deal'. Continuously seek God first by committing all your plans to Him and He will direct you in the path of success far beyond what you have asked. He did it to King Solomon who sought for wisdom and was also rewarded with wealth, possessions and honor.

As Meister Eckhart observed, "if the only prayer you said in your whole life was, "thank you," that would suffice". When you develop a heart of gratitude, you will see one door open after the other, and you will move from one level of glory to another.

PART I

The Basic Foundation

ജ്ഞ

CHAPTER 2

Establishing Your Vision

"Vision is the art of seeing what is invisible to others"

Jonathan Swift ~

God has destined you for greatness. However, you can choose to live and enjoy your comfort zone, everyday going to your place of employment or business and never experience the fullness of God's promises over your life. It is not uncommon to live 'one day at a time' with no plan or long term goal to achieve. As a result we fail to appropriately utilize the resources and the potential that God has given us.

It is never too late to discover the plan that the Lord has over your life. Nevertheless, the earlier in life you discover your purpose, the more time you'll have to pursue it and live life with contentment.

God's plan for you can be realized through a divine connection between your mind and God's mind, your spirit and God's Spirit, your heart and God's heart, your will and God's will, your desires and God's desires, during which there is a download of revelations from God's Spirit into your spirit.

This alignment between you and God leads to a perfect shift of your plans to God's plans. His plan for you is that each time He reveals a vision over your life; you accomplish it for His own glory.

Your vision is the compass that guides you through the journey to your destiny.

A vision may be for a specific reason or season and may be short term or long term. When you discover your calling, you develop a sense of completeness and satisfaction. You live in peace and are able to serve God and help others. However, most of us fall short of seeking God's vision over our life and end up pursuing a vision that is outside of God's will. We forget that unless God builds our dreams, all our efforts are futile.

As you go through the process of identifying your vision; ask God for knowledge and wisdom and know that God is not bound by any limit. Try not to put God's ability in a box called 'your life limitations', instead get out of that box and let the Lord direct you and you will discover the giant in you.

Purpose not to live 'life as usual' rather desire to live 'life unusual' by not limiting God. You are gifted in one way or another and all you need to do is to tap into what the Holy Spirit has freely given to you[1]. You will discover potentials that you never thought you had.

Though a vision is not necessarily something tangible, it is usually strategically set and works as a guiding light that provides direction into what you do. The bible clearly instructs us to have a vision. It lays down the consequences of not having any vision - people perish.

Your vision is basically an aspiration by God's grace towards an experience greater than what you are at this very moment. It is what you aspire to become or achieve. It is what you discern and an end-point which incorporates your values, dreams, and ambitions towards which all your goals are to be directed.

A vision works as a compass that guides you on the journey to your destiny. It ensures that you remain focused without deviating from the course you have set.

Season of Prayer and Waiting

The first step towards establishing your vision through Christ is to acknowledge Him and let Him have his way in your life. Let Christ take the driver's seat and let Him lead you. He has a plan for you to have a future full of hope and success in your entire endeavor. After acknowledging that He is in control; set aside a season that you will dedicate to prayers and waiting upon God's direction.

During this season make it a point to write down all

ideas that pass through your mind. Some thoughts may strike right in the middle of the night or in broad daylight or as you drive down the freeway, note them down as soon as you can.

These could be ideas of a project or things to accomplish, but take notes regardless of how simple they may seem to you. It could also be names of people who could potentially help you at one point to accomplish your vision. It could be a need or a gap that you identify in the community you live in or among those you interact with, or something you feel you need to communicate.

All these thoughts may not make sense to you as you write them down but continue to take note of them since they may form the foundation for your vision. *"Just as you cannot understand the path of the wind or the mystery of a tiny baby growing in its mother's womb, so you cannot understand the activity of God, who does all things."*[2] Our ways of seeing things are not the same as God's ways, and our timing is not God's timing. Therefore keep believing and writing down those ideas.

While You Wait

When you set out to pray, ask God for His will and then pray according to His will and calling. During this time be still and sensitive to His spirit. Listen to what He puts in your spirit. God wants you to come to Him so that you may reason together. By being in tune and connected to the spirit of God you will discern the right thing to do, the right time, the right place, and you will develop the right attitude.

God may be positioning you for a blessing but you could potentially miss it if you fail to move in God's timing. Make sure you don't miss your blessing. As you go to the Lord, be honest about every thought or idea you may have and be obedient to His directions. Be patient and take time to listen to what God has for you. Sometimes we are busy talking that we fail to listen or hear from Him.

As we will see later in the book, there is need for us to be patient and to persevere as we wait to hear from Him. He is full of compassion and will not turn a deaf ear to our cry; He will hear us if we patiently wait upon Him.[3] God's timing is always perfect even though we don't realize it at the time.

CONFIRMATION OF YOUR VISION

How do I know that God is leading me to a given direction regarding my vision? This is one of the many questions that we often ask ourselves as we seek God's direction.

Lack of a clear direction can be very confusing and frustrating. In order to step out in faith, you need to be confident that your vision is of God. God reveals His will to us in very diverse ways and as long as you are in tune with Him and obedient, you will not have difficulties identifying His voice and direction.

Confirmation through others

God may choose to use His servants to minister into our lives. You may get confirmation through sermons and teachings or through prophecy. In the entire scripture we see God using His servants to communicate with His people. He may also use others such as your family members, friends or people unknown to you.

You may see people just encouraging you to venture into a given area or speak a word into your life. In 2 Peter 3:15-16, we see Peter underscore Apostle Paul's ability in the ministry and the wisdom that God had given him.[4]

Prior to writing this book, I had people both in my social and professional networks that always encouraged me into writing books on various subjects. Though my experience was in scientific writings, it never dawned on me that God would use the same tool to fulfill my vision of writing a book.

When I was on the final stages of this book, I started getting confirmations from almost every teaching that I listened to. God started to use people to make comments on subjects that I was already working on. I took note and thanked God for the confirmation.

Always take note of any comments that are made about your ability. God may be using them to communicate His will for your life. God always has a purpose for every encounter you have with someone, but you need to discern it.

However, as we will see later in this chapter, be cautious about who and what you listen to and also with whom and what you share. Whatever others say should be in agreement with God's word and what He has already revealed to you.

Confirmation through gifts and talents

Confirmation of your vision could be in form of your God-given talents or gifts. God gives us gifts and talents to propagate and make use of. Do you have a talent or a gift of singing yet you choose to sit back? That may be your calling or the door to your blessing - go for it. Are you really creative at designing fliers, brochures and other graphics on your computer? Why don't you give a shot at graphic design?

Do what you can do best and not what others can or are doing. The problem with us is living in other people's dreams. Often we are tempted to do what our friends, family members or neighbors are doing without first seeking God for our own visions since we think that they are very successful.

Do what you can do to your best, not what others can or are doing.

Identify what talent or gift you have. God may use it as the door to usher you into your destiny. However do not let the talent or gift drive you, rather use them as pointers to what God may be leading you to. Be careful to use this for the glory of Him who has given you the gift.

It was not a coincident that Jesus chose His first disciples among the fishermen to be fishers of men. He knew what they were good at. Fishing!

Confirmation through your passion

Sometimes the zeal and the passion you have for something may be a clear indication of the direction that the Lord is leading you.

What excites you or what are you passionate about? Do you have a great desire to do this one specific thing? Do you find yourself doing some given task regardless of how much you try to suppress it? What can't you stand to see being done wrong? Do you see a relationship between your passion and your talents or skills? The Lord may be revealing your vision through your passion.

Confirmation through your personality

Your God-given character can be a lead to your vision. A combination of an honest assessment of your personal attributes, and your approach of issues may be a good pointer to your vision.

I do not know what experience you've had, but at one point my experience at a dentist local office made me long for my next visit to a pre-owned car lot.

The dentist found problems with almost each and every one of the thirty two teeth, and interestingly had a different solution for each one of them. It felt like an experience with a salesperson that finds fault with every aspect of your used car only to convince you into buying another pre-owned car.

There is nothing wrong with being a salesperson; they are just gifted with that convincing and persistent personality. They should put all their efforts into selling what they are tasked to sell.

Are you a natural extrovert who enjoys being around people? Or, are you good at entertaining people through a good sense of humor, or a good orator? This may be a lead for you to venture into the entertainment industry. Use your personality to do what you can do best. Whatever your character is, nurture it and use it to accomplish your vision.

Confirmation through personal situations

Sometimes events happen in our lives that God uses to communicate His will over us. Let's say for example that you have been pursuing that career for the last ten years, but have always been dissatisfied or miserable in all ways. And let's say you have prayed about it and sought God's guidance on the issue, but you still find yourself uncomfortable with your career.

This might be a hint that the Lord has another plan for you, seek it. God may be planning to use you in a different area. However, it is always wise to take time in prayer prior to making any step as such discomfort may be as a result of spiritual warfare.

Saul's encounter with Christ in Acts 9 is a great example of how God can change things around for His own glory. God used the encounter to change Paul's mission from self-centered independence to a God-centered mission that was dependent on God's direction.

As you face personal situations whether positive or negative, be in tune and attentive to the Holy Spirit; as God may be confirming a new direction over your life.

Confirmation through your skills

In some cases, your qualifications and skills may be all that you need to confirm your God-centered vision. You may have developed the skills either formally or informally to perform a given task or a given project.

We see Apostle Paul highlighting his zeal and also legal training and qualification under the leadership of Gamaliel.[5] God can use your skills as an avenue through which you can realize your vision.

As we have seen, there are endless ways through which God can use to confirm a vision for your life. The key is to listen to His voice and obey the directions that He gives you.

Through your vision, you will be in a position to take advantage of opportunities that come your way and will also deny the enemy an opportunity to devour you and your resources.[6] A vision reveals God's plan over your life and helps you to remain focused. Aim high and have a big vision.

Your blessings and provision will be proportional to your dream.

Your blessings and provision will be proportional to the dreams that you have. Do not despise yourself. It is not a matter of experience or what you have but a matter of what God can do through you.

The children of Israel were inexperienced slaves yet they drove out experienced armies from the Promised Land. Keep trusting, victory is on your way. God is working for you behind the scene. As I said earlier, He is positioning you for a blessing.

THE HABAKKUK PLAN

Once you have established your God-centered vision, summarize it into a two part plan that I refer to as *the Habakkuk plan.*

The first part of *the Habakkuk plan* should be a simple and plain statement that can be easily understood. In this part of the statement, you seek to explain what you intend to accomplish. It should reflect the principles of a vision as demonstrated in the scriptures by Prophet Habakkuk's vision. *"Write what you see. Write it out in big block letters so that it can be read on the run. This vision-message is a witness pointing to what's coming. It aches for the coming – it can hardly wait! And it doesn't lie. If it seems slow in coming, wait. It's on its way. It will come right on time."*[7]

Over the years I have realized the importance of writing down ideas. Writing helps them to stick. Start on your *Habakkuk plan* by drafting a very simple aspiration statement of what you want to accomplish. This is very similar to the answer that we all probably gave to our elementary school teacher when asked 'What do you want to be when you grow-up?'

Habakkuk's vision was to be made visible, that everyone who passes would be able to easily and quickly read it. This underscores the need for simplicity and clarity of your vision to an extent that you can clearly understand it.

A simple statement helps you to remain focused towards what you are just about to accomplish. Prophet Habakkuk was instructed to make his vision plain so that it can be read on the run. Although your vision may be plain, it needs to carry a lot of weight and reflect what you want to achieve.

This first part of *the Habakkuk plan* intentionally omits the details. These details would be incorporated on the second part of the plan.

The second part of *the Habakkuk plan* should give a broad and detailed outline of the vision that you intend to accomplish. It should define how you will measure any milestone attained. Here, you communicate both your purpose and values upon which you will build a detailed action plan.

Seek to highlight God's plan over your life by listing the details that you wrote down during the time you had set aside for prayers. You should include details of where you see yourself some years from now. At this point, you just describe the vision as you see it, but you are not setting goals.

Your vision may be simple but it will steer the great potential within you, to a great level of success.

Just as a simple rudder steers a mighty ship, or the bridle directs that fast-moving horse at the derby; your vision may be simple but it will steer the great potential within you to a great level success. Do not neglect having one; it may be the North Star that guides you and propels you forward towards your success.

Broadcasting your Vision

As much as broadcasting your vision may sound to be out of the norm, sharing the vision with someone you trust is very important. However, it is crucial for you to protect your dreams by carefully choosing who you reveal your vision to. You do not share your vision to get thumbs up or confirmation from others.

You should share your vision with only a few trusted people who will hold you accountable; support you in achieving your goal, and be a testament to what the Lord can do. You ought to share with people who will pray with you and challenge you to continue working on your vision. Sharing with people who motivate and encourage you will help you to see the tangible side of your dreams that makes your vision real.

When I first thought of writing this book, I shared the idea with a friend. This friend positively challenged me every time we met to an extent that he would call me while travelling overseas to check on the progress of the book.

Beware who you share your vision with. If you share your vision with negative people, chances are that they will discourage you and show you how difficult it is to achieve the task. Their message may become very venomous to your enthusiasm.

Exposure to such kind of negativity can easily be distractive and lead you to doubt your vision and the potential that the Lord has given you. Some of them may even want to take advantage of your vision, and want to live your dream.

In the bible, we read of the story of Joseph and how his own brothers hated him more when he shared his dreams with them that they formulated a plan to get rid of him.[8] Also, watch out not to share with people who may be out to sabotage your vision. These are the people who will work day and night to see that you fail in what you do.

Apostle Paul in 2 Timothy 4:14-15 is warning us to be on the guard against such people like Alexander, the coppersmith who did Paul *"great wrongs. The Lord will pay him back for his actions. Beware of him yourself, for he opposed and resisted our message very strongly and exceedingly."*[9]

Carefully speaking out your vision helps make it happen deep within you. Therefore speak it and you will believe it.

Visualize your Vision

As you start to work on your vision, picture your goals as if you have already achieved them. By visualizing your vision, you will be in a good position to define the tasks and the goals necessary to achieve the vision.

You can never become that which you criticize

Confess it aloud to yourself several times a day and believe that this is already happening in your life. This is the same principle we use when we convert and decide to follow Christ. You have to believe and confess it with your mouth.

By faith, believe that you will reach your goal regardless of the obstacles that you might face. Remember this is not your working; you are just a vessel through which God has chosen to use to accomplish His purpose. With this in mind, be confident that you can do all things through Him who strengthens you and as long as you believe that, success is certain.

In the book of Genesis 37, we see Joseph repeating

his dreams in great details and they came to pass. If God has put a vision in your heart, do not turn back. Be careful not to criticize that which you aspire to become, or those who have already achieved what you long to achieve. If you badly want God to bless you with something, you can't go around criticizing it or else you can't be it -- you cannot be what you criticize.

Gather Information Pertinent to your Vision

"Intelligent people are always ready to learn. Their ears are open for knowledge."[10] Gathering information is a very important aspect of working towards your vision.

Once you have established your vision, seek knowledge and skills necessary to accomplish it. This may mean enrolling for training classes to strengthen your skills or just general information pertinent to your vision. Learn by networking with people who have been successful in pursuing similar goals.

Take time and identify a mentor who can help you navigate through your vision. Seek to be a lifelong learner as this will help you gain knowledge and understanding of your vision, before, during and after the accomplishment. All skills can be learnt, don't let your dream be destroyed by lack of knowledge.[11]

Determine what is pertinent to your vision and pursue it. This will help you to develop personally and also professionally. It will help you save time and resources when you start to implement your vision.

Application Suggestion

1) What are some of the ways through which the Lord is confirming your vision?

"Your vision is an aspiration by God's grace towards an experience greater than what you are at this very moment"

ഇഗ

CHAPTER 3

Aligning Your Vision

"True freedom is where an individual's thoughts and actions are in alignment with that which is true, correct, and of honor - no matter the personal price"

~ Bryant H. McGill ~

Just as there are several ways through which the Lord can confirm your vision, so are there diverse ways in which your vision will affect you and those around you. It is therefore important for you to evaluate your God-given vision and ensure that it is not in conflict with other responsibilities that have been bestowed on you.

It is not uncommon to find ourselves neglecting

stewardship of other areas that the Lord has mandated us to be responsible for in order to pursue our own visions. To avoid any antagonistic pursuit of goals, you need to make sure that your vision is aligned with your family values, the ministry where the Lord has called you to serve, your spiritual values, and also your social and professional circles.

Occasionally you may need to take your vehicle to a mechanic for alignment service. Driving a vehicle that is out of alignment will require more energy input and effort to keep it from going off the road. Just as alignment is important in helping your vehicle remain on track, so is the alignment of your vision.

Failure to align your vision could potentially lead you off track and probably lead to a crash between your vision and other aspects of your life. Consequently, it might end up being too costly or challenging to restore and get back on track.

It is therefore important that you evaluate your vision to ensure that it is aligned with all other aspects of your life and areas that God has entrusted you to oversee. Your vision and your other God-given responsibilities should be complementary to each other.

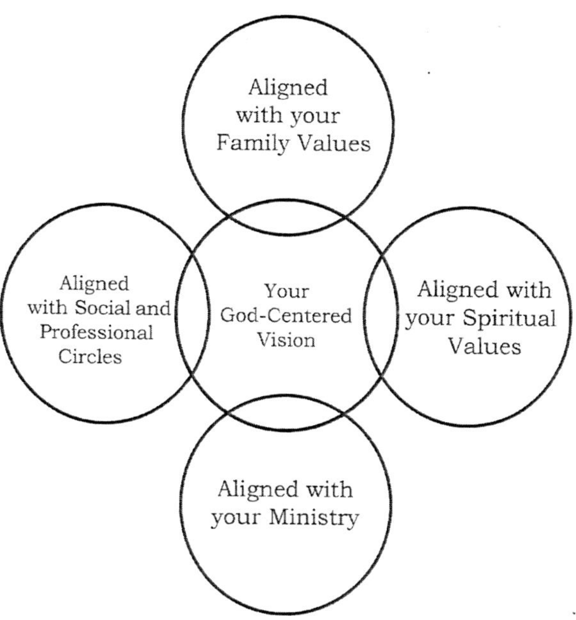

Aligned with your Family Values

A family is the basic unit of the church. Your most significant assignment is to take care of your family. Therefore, your vision should be aligned with your family values, and the two should not be in conflict.

As a leader of your vision, you need to live by the qualities depicted by Apostle Paul in 1Timothy 3 for someone who ought to be entrusted with leadership. The person to be assigned the responsibility of church leadership should be capable of managing his own family.

Pursuing our own goals whether in the ministry, business or otherwise with complete disregard of our family and family's goals, shows poor leadership in our part. You should never pursue your vision at the expense of your family. It is usually very painful to see someone neglect their family values in pursuant of their personal goals.

Unfortunately, it is not uncommon to see individuals tend to their church ministries or businesses at the expense of their families. This often results in absentee parenting leading to lack of Godly role models for children, and in worst cases, a breakdown of the family.

Your personal goals and your family goals or values should be in harmony and not in competition with one another. Make all efforts to ensure that your vision complements your family values and avoid conflicting goals. They should both be geared towards pleasing the Lord. Both your vision and your family are God-given and you should strive to be a good steward of the Lord's blessings.

Aligned with your Spiritual Values

Stick to your values and beliefs no matter what. Your goals must always be in agreement with your spiritual convictions.

In some instances, we face situations in which our goals antagonize our values. For example, you may have a goal to venture into a business or a career that perhaps involves some aspects that will conflict with your faith and impede you from any chance to witness to friends, colleagues, or clients.

I remember a story of a young family a few years ago trying to venture into business. An opportunity had opened for them to own a franchise, which among other things required that they stock liquor and cigarettes.

Though the business sounded very promising, it was completely in conflict with their spiritual values. They found out that there was no way they would have effectively witnessed to or helped a customer or a friend struggling with alcoholism.

You may lack the moral authority to challenge someone's personal life; but if you decided to own that corner pub, would you ever be comfortable witnessing to or helping an alcoholic? Would you tell a lie to win that lucrative business deal?

We need to ask ourselves which one is more important; our faith and belief or our goals. This takes me back to chapter two where we discussed about establishing a God-centered vision. If you have a God- centered vision, always stick to your faith.

Stick to your values and beliefs no matter what.

Your faith and your vision should not be in conflict. Think of Joseph and the cunning approach by Potiphar's wife. Joseph would have opted to give in to the temptation, sleep with Potiphar's wife hoping that the close relationship would usher him to leadership sooner. However, Joseph chose to remain firm to his moral values and faith and he rejected the temptation. Though Joseph was sent to prison, he came out victorious and became second in command.[1]

When we firmly stick to our faith, the Lord will promote us and expand our boundaries even as our enemies watch. He prepares a table for us in the presence of our enemies. Remain firm and you will be full of joy and enthusiasm as you work on your vision.

Aligned with your Ministry

Your vision should also balance with any other ministry work that God has entrusted you with. Perhaps you have been called to serve at your local church; use the skills that God has given you to serve Him. Do not let your vision lead you to compromise your service to God, rather use it to edify His Kingdom. Let your personal vision and that of your family be aligned with the work of God.

There are dangers of missing this alignment. We learn of the importance of this kind of alignment in Acts 5, in the story of Ananias and his wife, Sapphira and their real estate transaction. Both Ananias and Sapphira had their personal visions very well aligned with their family vision to an extent that they conspired to test the Spirit of God. They decided to deceive the Holy Spirit by inaccurately reporting their earnings on the piece of property that they had sold.

The story shows that they were in agreement in what they did. Their vision was however not aligned with that of the work of God. Consequently, the failure to align their family vision with that of the work of God led to their death.

When you fail to align your goals with that of your spiritual family or your calling, you may find yourself torn between family and ministry. Does one member of the family want to tithe or give towards the ministry while the other one is not willing?

Using the scriptures, make all efforts to align your goals and those of your family with those of the ministry where you are serving the Lord.

Aligned with your Social and Professional Circles

Your vision will have an impact on those around you; and those around you will have an impact on your vision. As the saying goes, 'no man is an island'. You cannot execute your vision in isolation. Let the Lord show you how you can be a blessing to those that you interact with and also how God can use them to help you accomplish your vision.[2]

Be proactive and expand your social and professional networks. This can be achieved through social or professional interactions as we will see later in the book. As you work on your goals, develop social contacts by participating in community activities, may it be church activities, school activities or other community events. This will not only renew your motivation and eliminate fatigue, but it will also open doors for you to meet new contacts that may help you accomplish your vision.

God may also use your professional contacts to help you move your vision to the next level. Surround yourself with big thinkers and people of faith, but be weary of people who can talk you out of your dream. Carefully choose under whose counsel you walk. Choose to hang out with the wise and you shall be wise, but as the scriptures say, if we walk in the company of fools we shall be destroyed.[3]

Surrounding yourself with doubters may cause a delay in your promises. As you walk with the wise, accept to be challenged especially if their goal is to build you. Learn from the challenges and constantly seek to improve yourself and increase your knowledge and understanding.

When your personal ambitions are aligned with God's plan; and the resulting God-centered vision is in alignment with your other areas of stewardship; you are more likely to be on target when you employ the principles described in this book.

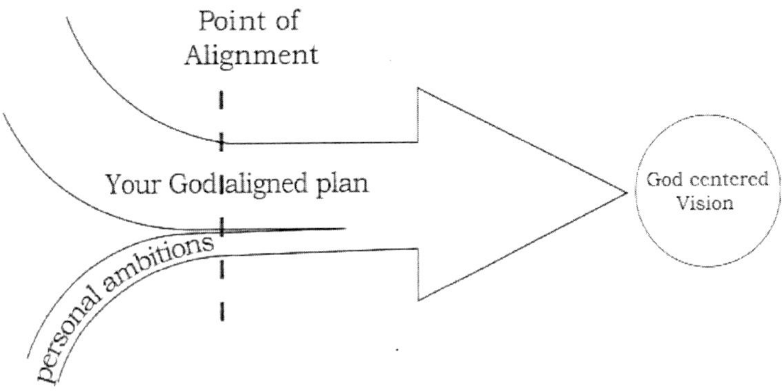

Now that you have established a God-centered vision, the next step is to build a strong foundation so that your vision can stand the test of time. In the next chapter, we will look into ways through which you can further develop your vision by building a strong foundation.

Application Suggestion

1) In what ways is your vision aligned with:-

a) Your family values?
b) Your ministry?
c) Your social and professional circles?
d) Your spiritual values?

"Just as alignment is important in helping your vehicle remain on track, so is the alignment of your vision with God's plan"

ഇരു

CHAPTER 4

Building the Foundation

"The foundation stones for a balanced success are honesty, character, integrity, faith, love and loyalty"

~ Zig Ziglar ~

Prior to working on your goals, it is important that you lay a firm foundation upon which you will build your vision. A vision built on faith, patience, courage and trust in God is like a house built on a solid rock; a strong foundation that cannot be destroyed when the wind blows or the floods come. These virtues coupled with resilience and your determination to take risk will drive your vision to success even in the dark times.

You have probably noted that the higher a sky-scraper rises, the deeper the foundation on which it is built. In the same manner, the depth to which you lay the foundation of your vision will determine the height to which the vision will rise. This strong foundation will help you to stand firm and will rejuvenate your motivation and hope when faced with challenges.

Have Faith and Trust in God

There is no better way to start building a strong foundation than to have faith in God and consult Him at every stage of your project. The entire eleventh chapter of the book of Hebrews gives an account of the faith of mighty servants of God.

Through faith we develop a strong conviction or belief that something is true and reliable beyond any reasonable doubt even when there is no tangible proof. This means that you totally embrace the promises that God has for you with absolute certainty even when reality dictates otherwise.

With faith you will go beyond hope or your personal ambitions, and you will have the conviction that God will do all that He says He will do. You can do this by taking God at His word and believing that He will bless the work of your hands. Unlike hope, your faith can increase.

In the scriptures, we see our faith being compared to a mustard seed. A mustard seed, just like any other seed can be propagated and grown to maturity. This principle is in fact used in the scriptures to illustrate the growth of the kingdom of God. In the same manner your faith can increase if you keep on believing God without doubt. What the Lord wants from us is that faith as small as a mustard seed, with the potential to grow.

Faith and Planning

As you start planning and executing your vision; seek God's guidance and have faith that through His strength you will do it. Above all, obey the directions that He gives you and believe with no doubt or double mindedness that you have what it takes to achieve your vision. The scriptures warn that a person who wavers should not expect to receive anything from the Lord.[1]

Sometimes the task may seem to be very enormous and challenging to your personal being such that you start to doubt your ability to handle it or wonder whether you really heard from the Lord. In such cases, do not give up; your faith will help you overcome the fear that hinders you from pursuing your vision.

In Matthew 21:20-22, we read of Jesus cursing the fig tree that was not bearing fruits. He put forward a challenge to his disciples that if they had faith and did not doubt; they too could do similar things and much more. And to show the disciples that nothing was above their limit, He said to them that with prayer and faith a mountain would obey their command to move and be lifted up and thrown into the sea.

God wants you to have faith in Him and He will in turn empower you as you face the task ahead. All that the

Lord is looking for is that genuine little faith. It is through that faith that He will work miracles in your life.

The woman with the issue of blood in Matthew 9 knew that if she only touched the helm of Jesus garment, she would be whole. The scripture says that her faith made her well and her health was restored to fullness. Her faith was manifested by trusting God through her actions and thoughts.

As you grow in faith, run to God your refuge and learn to take Him at His own word. *"Lean on, trust in, and be confident in the Lord with all your heart and mind and do not rely on your own insight or understanding. In all your ways know, recognize, and acknowledge Him, and He will direct and make straight and plain your paths."*[2] Keep on trusting, Jesus is presenting your case to the Father and he will see you through.

Cultivate your Patience

In the current world where everything seems to be fast-paced, it is not surprising that most people find it hard to develop patience. We have become a society that is so much used to instant things - instant coffee, instant tea, fast food and so on, that we want our prayers to be answered instantly or our projects to pick up and succeed instantly.

The truth of the matter is that, just as a vehicle takes time to pick up speed, so also will your vision take time to pick up speed. You do not start a car at a speed of seventy miles per hour; you need that acceleration lane to the freeway as you gain and pick up full speed.

You may start slow, but be patient when your life is

not moving as fast as you would like it to since you have not yet attained your maximum capacity. Your horsepower is not yet maxed out! This is especially so during the planning and preparation stages of executing your vision when most activities are 'behind the scene'.

The scriptures talks of the promise that God gave to Abraham that he will be a father of many nations.[3] God made this promise when Abraham was advanced in age and Sarah was past childbearing age. By faith Abraham patiently waited and from him came descendants as numerous as the stars in the sky and as countless as the sand on the seashore. God's promises on your life may tarry but be patient as they will be fulfilled.

The Lord also warned the Israelites to be patient with Him as they prepared to occupy Canaan. He warned them that though He was to drive their enemies out of the land; He expected their patience since He would *"not drive them out in a single year, because the land would become desolate and the wild animals would multiply and threaten you. I will drive them out a little at a time until your population has increased enough to take possession of the land."*[4]

Just as a farmer sow the seeds, patiently waits for the rains and watches as the crops grow to maturity; be patient, it may take you a little bit longer as the Lord prepares you or the conditions for you to reap the maximum benefits of your vision. The time you spend waiting upon the Lord is never wasted time.

Think and Talk Positive

Positive thinking and optimism feeds your mind with an attitude of belief. Your thoughts and confessions can either be a great asset or a huge liability to your vision. Cultivating a positive mindset is an essential motivating factor that will help build your faith.

As I discussed earlier, when you talk about your vision, do not criticize the same vision that you have believed God to bless you with. Whatever you confess can either build or destroy your vision.

Your thoughts and confessions can either be a great asset or a huge liability to your vision

It is not uncommon for people to criticize others for buying high-end property, yet they are trusting God to be blessed with the same. How would God entrust you with something that you criticize? You can never become that which you criticize. Think and talk positive about what is in your heart as any negativity may drive you out of your own miracle.

In Philippians 4:8, Apostle Paul implores us to be optimistic and feed our minds with positive thoughts by *"meditating on things true, noble, reputable, authentic, compelling, gracious – the best, not the worst; the beautiful, not the ugly; things to praise, not things to curse."*[5] These are all attributes of a positive thinker. This is what Paul elsewhere calls the renewal of your mind that helps you discern what is good, acceptable and the perfect will of God.[6]

Improve your positive thoughts by making all efforts not to confess defeat but the victory that comes from Christ Jesus. You should not let your own tongue kill your dreams.

Gather Courage

As Maya Angelou indicated, courage is one of the most important virtues. Most of us seek God for direction over our life and go to an extent of setting goals; but at the end we lack the courage to stand to the challenge and often fail to take that first step towards our vision.

It takes courage to depart from our comfort zone into a territory unknown to us. For you to overcome the fear that holds you back from reaching your potential; you'll need to take courage and step out into the unknown.

Sometimes you may feel as if you lack the experience or you are not adequately equipped to pursue your vision or a given goal; but as we saw earlier, the children of Israel were inexperienced slaves yet they drove out experienced armies from the Promised Land. It is not a matter of experience, but the courage to face the challenge. If you do not have the courage to tackle the challenges that you face in pursuant of your vision, those challenges may distract you from achieving your goals at a later stage.

Benaiah Son of Jehoiada

One of my pastor's favorite bible stories is the account of a courageous man called Benaiah. Benaiah was the son of Jehoiada, a fearless warrior from Kabzeel. He is said to have done many heroic deeds, which included killing two of Moab's mightiest warriors. But one of his most courageous deeds was to chase a lion down into a pit, caught it and killed it.[7] To go after such a beast took courage. Think of an encounter with a grizzly bear as you hike at Yellowstone National Park, a Siberian tiger or an African Lion in the Savannah. These cats are large and fierce, yet we see Benaiah not only chasing the lion but also catching it and killing it.

He did this at a time when the conditions were not conducive for the encounter. The scripture says that the ground was covered with snow and was slippery. Having lived in the upper Mid-west most of my adult life, I know how harsh it is to be outside on a snowy day, let alone have an encounter with a lion.

When you go after your goals, the challenges may seem too huge for you to overcome or the conditions may not be very conducive; but as Jesus indicated in the parable of the mustard seed, it is not about the greatness of your faith or the size of your problem, but it is the absence of doubt that moves the heart of God. Keep trusting, your help may come from the most unlikely source.

It is not a matter of experience, but the courage to face the challenge.

Mighty Men of David

In the books of 2 Samuel and 1 Chronicles, we see David's mighty men described as men of courage. Josheb-basshebeth is said to have stood up to several hundred of the enemies and killed all of them in a day while Eleazar seems to have been defending a field full of barley, which the Philistines may have intended to plunder or destroy. Shammah on the other hand stood his ground when the people fled from the Philistines. The Lord gave him victory against the

Philistines.[8,9]

The qualities of these mighty men of David encourage us to have courage and to stand our ground against any attack and in defense of the resources and the vision that the Lord has given us. You must have courage to pursue your dreams in spite of the conditions. Most of the times we tend to run away from the challenges instead of overcoming the situation.

Benaiah would have opted not to go after the lion as soon as it got into the pit, but he chose to face it in the pit.

All the odds may be stacked up against the achievement of your goals, but don't give up. *"Be strong. Take courage. Don't be intimidated. Don't give them a second thought because GOD, your God, is striding ahead of you. He's right there with you. He won't let you down; he won't leave you."*[10]

Be prepared to face detractors when in pursuit of your vision. Nehemiah faced ridicule from detractors who said that the wall he was building was so weak that it would tumble down in ruins again if a fox tried to walk on it. Nehemiah and his workers paid no attention to the jokes and jeer but remained focused and the Lord gave them success (Nehemiah 4).

Remember that the Lord is saying *"when you go to war against your enemy and see horses and chariots and soldiers far outnumbering you, do not recoil in fear of them; GOD, your God, who brought you up out of Egypt is with you."*[11] As Alexander the Great said "I am not afraid of an army of lions led by a sheep; I am afraid of an army of sheep led by a lion." Discover the leader in you, have courage and take charge, for the Lord is with you.

Develop Resilience

Resilience is your ability to rise up the eighth time after seven falls. It is the ability to recover from the challenges and setbacks that you encounter as you execute your vision. You've probably heard the idiom 'every cloud has a silver lining' being used to mean that you can always draw some benefit from every weakness or hardship you encounter. This means that as you execute your vision; you will face challenges and setbacks that if properly handled; and leveraged can be turned into strength.

Circumstances may push you to the limit, with one challenge coming after the other, or you may feel inadequate; do not give up in your endeavor. With resiliency, these challenges and setbacks will usher you into a greater level of dependence on God's strength.

Resilience is your ability to rise up the eighth time after seven falls.

When one challenge knocks you down, depend on His strength and rise up. The enemy may think that you are done; but at that dark moment, run unto the Lord your strong tower and you will emerge victorious. When you think you are weak, you are strong.

It was during the darkest hour of Christ's crucifixion that His power was manifested in the entire land and witnessed by those who had rejected His cause. *"And at once the curtain of the sanctuary of the temple was torn in two from top to bottom; the earth shook and the rocks were split."*[12] Those who crucified Him thought that this was His weakest moment, yet God had already planned that this was the moment to save mankind.

With resilience, you will bounce back higher than you ever did before.

Embrace What God has Given Even if it is Unknown to you

In most cases when God directs us to complete a task, we develop fear of approaching the unknown. We forget that God is all knowing and that He has our destiny in His hands. In Genesis 12, God approached Abraham and told him to leave his country, his relatives and his father's house and go to a land that the Lord was to show him. That meant that God wanted Abraham to leave his comfort zone and venture into the unknown.

Sometimes we want to know the details of how everything will work out. God wants you to believe when you hear His promises and take a step of faith even when the destination is not certain. He wants us to leave our comfort zone. It is our responsibility to embrace the uncertainty because God knows with absolute certainty that the Promised Land is on the other side.

When angel Gabriel appeared to Mary in Luke 1, to proclaim the good news that she was to give birth to a son and call him Jesus; Mary's first reaction was to wonder how that could be, yet she was a virgin. Mary wanted to have more details on how that was possible, but the angel's response was that the Holy Spirit and the Most high God was in control.

Sometimes we may face surprises on the direction

that the Lord is leading us, but we should always embrace what He has for us and not worry about the fine details on how He will accomplish it.

Take the Risk

Facing any project will involve taking some level of risk. What do I mean? You do not know the outcome of the work you are undertaking, only God does. However, the cost of not starting that project might be greater than that of starting the project. The Lord who knows the count of the hair on your head and feeds all the birds of the air will take care of you.

You have probably faced a situation in which risking was inevitable but chose not to risk. In some cases choosing not to risk is not fruitful. I tried not to risk, but that didn't work very well for me. I therefore made a decision to risk than not risk at all. You would rather risk since you have faith in Christ. It is never too late to gather courage; take the risk and make a radical change in your life. Do not be afraid to break the cycle of fear.

Challenges and setbacks will usher you into a greater level of dependence on God's strength.

In the story of Esther and Mordecai, Mordecai advised Esther not to be afraid of taking risk, saying; "*Don't think that just because you live in the king's house you're the one Jew who will get out of this alive. If you persist in staying silent at a time like this, help and deliverance will arrive for the Jews from someplace else; but you and your family will be wiped out. Who knows? Maybe you were made queen for just such a time as this.*"[13] God has a plan for you and He will not let you go through what you cannot handle.

When I was learning how to swim, I was always scared of the deep end of the pool until I once decided to take the risk and swim towards the deep end. Since then, swimming has never been the same again. Though risky, swimming at the deep end may just be what you need to tap and enjoy what God has put in your heart - Get in and take the risk.

Peter, the disciple of Jesus took a risk and obeyed Jesus call to walk on the water.[14] He took the risk because he knew that this was a call from Jesus who was on the other side. Take the risk and jump into the waters; the Lord is holding you with His hand and will not let you submerge. By taking the risk, you gain access to the supernatural.

Application Suggestion

1) List five promises from the bible that you intend to use as a source of encouragement as you pursue your vision:-

a)

b)

c)

d)

e)

"Faith is embracing God's promises with absolute certainty even when reality dictates otherwise"

PART II

Weighing the Options

ജ്ഞ

CHAPTER 5

Discovering the Rod

"Success is achieved by developing our strengths, not by eliminating our weaknesses"

~ Marilyn vos Savant ~

Now that you have built the foundation of your vision through faith in God, seek to understand what the Lord has put in you. More often than not we fail to acknowledge who we are in the Kingdom. We need to understand that God has given each one of us a special gift, talent or strength that we can leverage as we work towards our vision. Similarly, we may have some areas that are dull and need to be sharpened.

This is what the corporate world would call SWOT analysis or determination of your strengths, weaknesses, opportunities and threats as we will discuss in the next two chapters.

By assessing our strengths, weaknesses, opportunities and threats we will be able to build the faith we have in God into confidence and consequently to a strong foundation. "*But don't begin until you count the cost. For who would begin construction of a building without first calculating the cost to see if there is enough money to finish it? Otherwise, you might complete only the foundation before running out of money, and then everyone would laugh at you. They would say, 'There's the person who started that building and couldn't afford to finish it!*"[1]

Just as any handyman assembles his or her tools prior to engaging in any work, so should you also be prepared by determining what you have prior to starting any task. You need to sit back and find out what 'tools' God has provided and what support you need to get from your sphere of influence.

Identify your Strengths

The scripture reminds us that we can do all things through Him who strengthens us and to seek the LORD and His strength. Knowing that your strength comes from the Lord, take your position and acknowledge who you are today. What do you have? What can the Lord use to accomplish your vision? Accept the truth about yourself as this will help you in your planning.

We learn of the rod that God asked Moses and Aaron to use as God prepared them to rescue the Israelites from Egypt. They used the rod on several occasions as they faced Pharaoh but the one instant most often told of is when Moses used the rod to split the red sea and to turn it into dry land. *"So God said, "What's that in your hand?" "A staff" "Throw it on the ground." ….. "God said to Moses: "Why cry out to me? Speak to the Israelites. Order them to get moving. Hold your staff high and stretch your hand out over the sea: Split the sea! The Israelites will walk through the sea on dry ground."*[2]

The Rod in Your Hands

In this story, God used the rod that Moses already had in his hands. Just as was the case with Moses, God wants you to identify what is in your hands. He wants you to know that He has already placed a staff or a rod in your hand that He can readily use to accomplish your vision and catapult you to greater heights. Determine what talents, gifts, skills or other resources you have that you can commit towards your vision.

You have a rod in your hand that the Lord is ready to use.

Previously in the same story of Moses, when God called him at the burning bush to go and deliver the Israelites from Egypt; Moses gave all kinds of excuses as to why he was not the right person to send. He excused himself as not having what it takes to accomplish the task. What Moses did not know is that God knew who he (Moses) was, what he had, and how He (God) was to use him to execute the plan.

At the burning bush, God identified Himself to Moses, as *"I Am who I AM"* meaning that He is the same God of Abraham, Isaac, and Jacob, the one that never changes.[3] He would be with him and the Israelites just as He was with their forefathers. God wanted to show Moses that this was not his project but God's plan and that Moses was just a vessel available for God's use.

In the same way, as you plan to execute your vision know that the Lord is with you. You are his vessel to accomplish the task that He has given you.

Do not be worried or concentrate on your inadequacies. Focus on what you have as the Lord will be your provider. Moses tried to give excuses of lack of eloquence or previous speaking engagements. But the Lord answered him that it is He who gives the ability to speak and commanded him to proceed.

As you plan to execute your goals, don't look down on yourself. God has placed boundless potential in you that He can use to accomplish your vision. *"Do not neglect the gift which is in you, [that special inward endowment] which was directly imparted to you [by the Holy Spirit]."*[4] Choose to work hard towards your vision and soon you will realize that as you put more effort, you will gain more experience leading to greater accomplishments.

Ways to Identify Your Strengths

Identify your strengths by:

- Discovering your talents and gifts.
- Identifying the skills or resources that you have or have the ability to acquire.

- Being keen on what people say you are good at.
- Discovering what you constantly do differently compared to those around you.
- Identifying what you are passionate about.

Identify What Opportunities are Available to you

Identify the opportunities available to you and seize them. Ephesians 5:16 implores us to make the most of every opportunity and not to waste time on work that is not fruitful. God will always provide opportunities for you to take advantage of, to achieve your vision. It is up to you to be in tune with the Holy Spirit and discern what is on the table for you. Winners discern opportunities that are not obvious to the ordinary man.

You may identify opportunities by:

- Identifying an unmet need either in your life, family, community or any other area that you may have influence.
- Identifying a niche that you can make the most of.
- Being current on what is going on in the world around you. This could be in form of reading the current literature.
- Determining and taking advantage of available and untapped resources. For example you can take advantage of college scholarships, grants for start-up projects, employer based retirement programs and tuition reimbursement programs to retool or gain new skills.

- Networking and connecting with people who have pursued or are in the process of pursuing similar goals. Use this to harness the strengths of those who have already achieved what you are trying to achieve.
- Getting out and volunteering in leadership positions in your community. For example by participating in church and school boards or your local council government.
- Joining professional organizations and business clubs.

Sometimes we miss God's blessings by not being cognizance of the opportunities that we encounter. Seek to create opportunities that align with your purpose. The window of opportunity may be very small, but if you are in tune with God and do not disregard any pertinent information that comes your way, you will not miss that window.

Be attentive to what those around you say, for *"the wise also will hear and increase in learning, and the person of understanding will acquire skill and attain to sound counsel [so that he may be able to steer his course rightly]"*[5]

Lesson from Joseph

Opportunities may come in multiple forms. You may have read the story of Joseph the dreamer (Genesis 37) and dream interpreter (Genesis 41) who while in prison became a dream consultant and helped his fellow inmates. As a consultant, he helped interpret Pharaoh's dreams and offered him a plan on how to approach the seven years of hunger that would follow the seven years of abundance. Joseph made good use of every opportunity; he became very good in dream consulting that Pharaoh put him in-charge of executing the dreams. [6]

Just as Joseph made the most of the opportunities that arose, so should you also be sensitive to the Holy Spirit as multiple opportunities may open up for you to pursue. This is encouraging especially when you have multi-faceted talents, gifts or skills, and you are wondering which one to pursue. In fact the bible encourages us to pursue multiple opportunities for we do not know which one will succeed. [7]

Application Suggestion

1) What strengths will you seek to leverage in your vision?
2) What available opportunities will you seek to leverage in your vision?

"Winners discern opportunities that are not obvious to the ordinary man"

ꕥ

CHAPTER 6

Sharpening the Dull Blade

"An optimist sees an opportunity in every calamity; a pessimist sees a calamity in every opportunity"

~ Winston Churchill ~

Just as every calamity can be turned into an opportunity, every weakness can be turned into strength. We all have limitations or what I refer to as dull areas that may need to be sharpened. However, most people fail to assess their weak areas which subsequently impede the efforts to accomplish their vision. It is important that you evaluate your weaknesses and devise ways to overcome them with the understanding that you have a helper, the Holy Spirit who helps you in your weakness.

To identify areas of improvement, you need to get real and make an honest assessment of the areas that you might need help with. Identifying your limitations is a key aspect of planning as it will help you to quickly learn from them and determine what can be changed and what cannot. It also allows you determine what resources you need and how to allocate them.

In the previous chapter we looked at the story of the builder who wanted to build a house.[1] Jesus explained that a builder would first sit down and evaluate the cost of building to see if they have enough money to finish it. In other words, you will need to identify areas that you may not be sufficient.

Honestly evaluate your limitations and leverage the strengths of the people around you.

In the same scripture, Jesus talks of a king planning to go to war with another king. He says that the king would first sit down to establish if he is able to win with his ten thousand men fighting against the one who comes with twenty thousand. If he determines that he does not stand a chance to win, he would send a delegation and seek peace while the other is still a long way off.

In these two instances, the passage is helping us understand that we all have limitations and areas that need improvement. Albert Einstein is quoted to have said that "Everybody is a genius. But if you judge a fish by its ability to climb a tree, it will live its whole life believing that it is stupid." You are strong in your own way; don't judge yourself based on your weaknesses. Recognizing your limitations is acknowledging that you are not perfect and that you are ready to let go and let God the Omniscient take control.[2]

Strengthen your Weak Areas

Once you identify your weak areas, seek help and do not let the limitations haunt you or let the enemy take advantage of this. You are victorious in Christ. Give the Lord the opportunity to sharpen you through His word and also through others because just as *"Iron sharpens iron; so a man sharpens the countenance of his friend."*[3] All you need is to be honest about yourself and by doing so, you will be able to discern when the Lord speaks to you on how to address the issue. There are several ways in which you can leverage or strengthen your weak areas. For example, you may:

- Identify someone whose strength can complement your weaknesses.
- Seek training to develop the weak area.
- Find a mentor or a coach.
- Volunteer or work in an area that will help you gain the desired experience.
- Join a support group where you can learn skills and gain experience associated with the weakness.

One of the popular quotes on perceived weakness was from Michael Jordan, the all-time basketball star and hall of famer, who said that "My attitude is that if you push me towards something that you think is a weakness, then I will turn that perceived weakness into a strength".

The Lord can turn your perceived weakness into strength. Purpose to sharpen the blade since it is the value of wisdom that will help you succeed rather than use a dull axe that require more energy input.[4]

Leverage the Strengths of Those around you

It is important to leverage the strengths of the people in your social and professional circles to complement your weaknesses. In Exodus 4:27, God saw the sincerity in Moses, as he disclosed his limitation. In return God sent Aaron to him as a companion and a helper. In the same manner, you need to honestly evaluate your limitations and leverage the strengths of the people around you.

In most cases, the vision you have will take more than yourself to accomplish. You will need to surround yourself with people with whom you have confidence that they will be an asset and not a liability to your vision. These could be people that you trust in your social and professional networks. They are your foot soldiers who like the fighting men of David are willing to help you in pursuing your vision. They should:

- Understand your vision.
- Understand the timing.
- Have courage and be ready to support you no matter the circumstances.
- Be armed with necessary tools to help you succeed in your vision.
- Be fully determined to help you.

- Have the skills and knowledge.
- Be persistent.
- Be sensitive to the Holy Spirit.
- Be people who can hold you accountable.

Leverage the strengths of those around you; they can become your greatest asset to your vision.

Identify your Threats

Obstacles and threats that hinder you from achieving your goals will arise as you execute your vision. Identifying these threats will prevent you from being caught off-guard by unpleasant surprises. However, do not let these threats distract you, rather devise ways to overcome them or rebrand yourself. Use the threats as an opportunity for you to prepare, retool and strategize your plan of action.

Learn from them and remember the Lord has declared that in the *"coming day no weapon turned against you will succeed. You will silence every voice raised up to accuse you. These benefits are enjoyed by the servants of the LORD; their vindication will come from me."*[5]

The threats you face may be from external sources that you have no control over, or they may be threats that arise from your mindset or approach of certain things. A positive mindset will be a great tool to use when faced with threats. It will help you to realistically evaluate the threat and determine what approach to adopt in tackling it.

The scriptures in the book of Numbers chapters 13 and 14 gives a detailed account of the twelve spies that Moses sent to explore Canaan, the land that the Lord had given to the Israelites. Among the twelve were Joshua and Caleb.

The twelve explored the land and brought back the report. With exception of Joshua and Caleb, the other ten gave a report of a very good land that had very large and fortified cities with milk and honey, but whose inhabitants were powerful giants. They saw themselves as grasshoppers compared to the inhabitants of the land.

Joshua and Caleb on the other hand gave a report of a land that was exceedingly good flowing with milk and honey. In their report they saw the Lord leading them into that land where they would devour and overcome the inhabitants.

In this story, the twelve spies were presented with the same threat; they explored the same land and encountered the same challenges; however they gave very different accounts of their experience - different mindset, different reports.

As you evaluate these limitations and threats, see opportunities and not obstacles. Do not be distracted, rather maintain a balanced and proper perspective of your vision by focusing on ideas that you can potentially develop into viable concepts.

Application Suggestion

1) What are some of the areas that need improvement prior to working on your vision?
2) What are some of the threats you anticipate to face as you execute your vision?
3) What are the strengths of your social and professional networks?
4) How do you plan to leverage these strengths to accomplish your vision?
5) Write down five (5) key people that can support you in accomplishing your vision.

"Do not be worried or concentrate on your inadequacies. Moses had them yet he was victorious"

PART III

ঌ৫

From Ideas to Reality

ᘓᘐ

CHAPTER 7

Setting Your Goals

"The vision must be followed by the venture. It is not enough to stare up the steps - we must step up the stairs"

~ Vance Havner ~

Now that you have understood the factors to consider in establishing a God-centered vision and the keys necessary for building a strong foundation, I will walk you through the process of planning and goal setting. Goals are the roadmap to guide you in the right direction towards your vision. Attempting to accomplish a vision without setting clear goals is like setting out for a journey to a certain destination without a roadmap on how to get there. The process is just as important as the product.

God clearly demonstrated the process of planning when He created the universe and after the fall of man. After the fall of man, God as the Master planner began with the end in mind. He developed a redemption plan that would be realized thousands of years later through the birth, death and resurrection of Jesus Christ.

Since we are made in the image and likeness of God, we have an inherent ability to plan unless we choose not to exercise that ability. If God the Almighty took time to plan, how much more important is it for us to make efforts and plan for what we do.

The process is just as important as the product.

You may have come across one of the variants of the old British Army adage: The 7Ps (Proper Prior Planning and Preparation Prevents Poor Performance) or the 11Ps (Purpose, Proper Prior Planning, Passion, Patience, Persistence and Perseverance Prevents Poor Performance). If you carefully plan your goals, you will eliminate surprises when it comes to implementation.

As you plan your goals, ensure that they are God-centered and in alignment with your vision. Just acknowledge Him in all aspects of your planning and He will make our plans successful.[1] The Lord perfects the plans of those who put their hope and trust in Him.[2] That means if we develop God- oriented goals, then we are deemed to succeed. Man-centered goals on the other hand will fail as did the tower of babel.[3]

John Buchan, one of the great Scottish statesmen and

writer once said that "The task of leadership is not to put greatness into humanity, but to elicit it, for the greatness is there already". As you set your goals know that God has already instilled in you what it takes to accomplish them. Acknowledge His strength and know that you are a vessel honored to carry out the vision that is meant to bring glory to God.

Be careful not to exalt yourself. Above all pray that the Lord may guide you in the entire process for He has good plans for you. "*For I know the plans I have for you," says the LORD. "They are plans for good and not for disaster, to give you a future and a hope."*[4]

For you to properly plan and achieve your goals, you will need to take action and come out of your comfort zone. We see this in the character of Nehemiah as he went around the perimeter of the city of Jerusalem to inspect the ruined wall.[5] We should always actively engage ourselves in the process of planning and goal setting. God's sovereignty should not be interpreted to mean inactivity in our part.

During the planning stage of your vision, you should allow enough time to lay the foundation. This stage is usually not characterized by a lot of visible activities and it may seem as if nothing is going on. Be patient, and keep going. Just as the river makes the least noise where it runs the deepest; so will the impression be when you are in the process of building a deep and strong foundation for your vision.

Specific yet Flexible

Your goals need to be very specific. The more specific your goals are; the greater the chances that you will accomplish them. If your goals are very general, it is easy to lose the focus of your target. Though your goals should be specific, you should always be flexible and wait to hear from the Lord for directions. You should not be very rigid that you miss God's directions and blessings. That means you should be ready to be interrupted from the normal course you have set.

In Acts chapter 3:1-10, as Peter and John were headed to the temple, they allowed themselves to be interrupted and they attended to the needs of the paralytic by the gate Beautiful.

The word of God tells us to let our requests be made known to Him.[6] The Lord wants us to be specific in what we ask in prayers. The use of the term "requests" in this case emphasizes the specificity. When you 'request' something from someone, you must be specific. There is no blank request, but this does not mean that God does not already know what you need. He knows even before we ask.

Setting Specific Goals

There are a lot of passages in the bible that encourage us to be specific in what we do especially in prayer. For example Hannah who lacked ability to bear children asked God to bless her with a child and we see the Lord blessing her with a son. Hannah was specific in what she wanted, a male child; and God blessed her with Samuel.[7] King Hezekiah on the other hand knew that he was in the verge of death due to poor health. He asked the Lord to spare his life and God gave him fifteen extra years.[8] These are just a few examples of specific needs being petitioned to God.

In the same manner, we need to be specific in setting our goals.

- Be specific on the purpose of this goal. Why are you doing the task?
- Be specific on what active part you will play towards your goal(s) or what part 'you' as a family will play.
- Specify who else will be involved as you work towards accomplishing the goal.
- Have a specific timeline as to when you intend to start and finish the goal. This will help you over come procrastination.
- If accomplishing your goal involves identifying a location, then be specific about that. This is especially important if you intend to operate a business.
- Finally you need to be specific on how you are going to perform the task.

Clearly Understand the Cost

Setting goals alone is not enough; you will need to clearly understand what it takes to accomplish your vision. Do not run blindly but make sure that you understand the "do's and don'ts" of your project.

Evaluate all aspects of your vision to ensure that you clearly understand what you will need to accomplish it and what challenges you expect to encounter. *"It's best to stay in touch with both sides of an issue. A person who fears God deals responsibly with all of reality, not just a piece of it."*[9] This will help you efficiently manage the workload and the resources. It will also help you identify what you might need to forfeit.

Assessing the scope and what will be required to accomplish the vision may call for you to give-up something that you hold dearly in-order to achieve your goals. When Jesus called his first disciples, they had to give up their nets and fishing business to follow Him; you might need to give up that gadget or remote control or that trip to the shopping mall.

Clearly understand what it takes to accomplish your vision.

Measurable and Tangible Goals

Establishing a distinct criterion to regularly measure the milestones and the progress of your vision is very important. It offers a benchmark upon which you can gauge your achievements. It also gives you a chance to reflect on those achievements allowing you to have time to reevaluate and refocus your goals.

If you are involved in any given sport, you do not just play the game; you make all efforts to score as a measure of accomplishment. The players normally take a 'time out', and use that time not only to have a glimpse of the last play but mainly to use that last play to strategize, refocus and plan the next move. This helps to boost morale and motivate the player (s) to work even harder.

Your life milestones such as birthdays, weddings or anniversaries of important and special life events are often marked with celebrations. You observe these achievements by not only reflecting and learning from your past, but also focusing on the future.

In the story of creation, God created everything in the universe in six days. Upon completion, He looked and saw that everything He had made was very good. He marked the milestone on the seventh day by resting from all His work. Remember as you set your goals, designate measurable milestones and give glory to the one who has taken you that far.

The higher you set your goal the more motivated you will be to work towards achieving it.

Set goals that are tangible and those that can be marked by given milestones. They are goals that you can sense in one way or another using your sense of smell, hearing, taste, touch, or sight. These are good indicators of concrete goals and they help you identify your accomplishments.

Realistic and Attainable Goals

As we will see later in this book, it is important to identify the goals that are most important and relevant to your vision. By doing so, you will be able to prioritize them and begin to plan on ways to achieve them. The goals you set should be high enough yet attainable. They should represent a vision towards which you have the willingness and ability to work.

In Luke 14:31, we are told of the dangers of engaging in a project that is unattainable. *"What king would go to war against another king without first sitting down with his counselors to discuss whether his army of 10,000 could defeat the 20,000 soldiers marching against him?"*

Before you engage in a project, take time and determine what the project will entail. Determine what resources you currently have at hand and what you still need to acquire. In some cases we embark on projects that are not attainable.

Though you may have faith to move mountains; avoid setting goals that are not realistic. I do not doubt the word of God that you can do all things through Christ; but setting attainable goals is part of proper planning. God demonstrated this by taking six days to create the universe yet He is Omnipotent and would have opted to do it in a single day. This sets a good example of the importance of setting realistic and attainable goals.

Having said that, the higher you set your goal the more motivated you will be to work towards achieving it. You should break down major goals into smaller realistic tasks. By doing this you are more likely to succeed. If you set too low of a goal, then you will lack motivation to work on it and will keep procrastinating since the goal may not seem that important.

In some instances, you may find yourself setting unrealistic goals or trying to be a perfect achiever. Though it is not always a bad idea to set high expectations, more often than not you may fail to meet them and finally quit. As the saying goes "Aim at the sun to land on the moon", aim higher but be realistic.

Sometimes the roadblocks that you encounter may

hinder your progress but that does not mean that your goals are unrealistic or unattainable. It means that you need to be a little bit more persistent to the end. However, carefully monitor this because in some cases, you may not realize that your goals were very unrealistic until a time when you fail and probably quit.

Forty Days in November

Think of a young believer who in mid-November decides to fast for forty days and forty nights to seek the Lord for his or her spiritual life. I don't discount this to be impossible, but it is more likely that this young believer will give up by Thanksgiving or Christmas holidays. As much as this is a noble goal, the timing of the goal may not be appropriate and the goal may not be attainable for this individual.

In some cases we may become overzealous in trying to achieve monster goals instead of setting small and realistic goals that can be achieved in steps. Unrealistic goals will not only demoralize you but they can lead you to doubt your faith and abilities. If you find out that your goals are unrealistic and that you are not going to achieve them; seize that moment to reflect and readjust your strategy.

Break unrealistic and unattainable goals into small manageable tasks that you can easily achieve. Work within your capabilities and do not overwork yourself as this will be a recipe for a failed vision. Actually, the scripture implore us not to wear ourselves out *"trying to get rich. Be wise enough to know when to quit."*[10] This does not mean that we should not aim high; rather we should have realistic and attainable goals.

Hebrew 12:1-3 encourages us to run the race that is set before us with perseverance. Your goal can be high and yet realistic depending on how you set it. You are a partner with God in achieving it. He is the one who strengthens you; do not back away from high challenging goals, but be realistic.

Establish a Plan and a Timeline

Your goals should be accomplished in God's timing.[11] Having said this, setting definite dates of when you will work on a given task will be an important step in achieving goals.

Time frame creates a sense of urgency.

Establishing a timeline of events has been used in the bible from the story of creation in Genesis to the second coming of Christ in the book of Revelation. For example, during creation God made light and separated day from night. These clearly demarcated the seasons, the days, and the years. This shows that God's intent was for us to establish timelines in the tasks we do.

The genealogy of Christ as described in the book of Matthew shows God's plan for Jesus the Messiah.[12] We see a timeline across generations from Abraham to Joseph and Mary the mother of Jesus. Having a time frame creates a sense of urgency in achieving your goals. The time frame should not be set too far into the future because this is a recipe for loosing focus and interest.

The goals and the timing should be synchronized for you to remain motivated and excited. If the timing is too short, then chances are you will not complete your goal in a timely manner and this may cause frustrations.

Allocate enough time for planning and also for the actual activities. Do not just move to execution stage of your vision without spending time to sharpen your saw - to plan. If possible use the Pareto principle to allocate your time. First described in early 1900's by an Italian economist Vilfredo Pareto, this widely used 80/20 rule shows that about eighty percent of the outcome is as a result of twenty percent effort.

Dedicate 20% of your time and resources to achieving 80% of the relevant, urgent and important goals. This will help you review your progress, determine when milestones are to be accomplished, and set the completion date. You can set the timeline by noting them next to your goals; using a calendar or appropriate software.

You should also allow some time to reflect on past accomplishments and lay the ground for the next steps. This time should be used to seek God's directions and to readjust accordingly.

Remember that there is a time for everything, and a season for every activity under heaven; God *"changes the seasons and guides history, He raises up kings and also brings them down, he provides both intelligence and discernment, He opens up the depths, tells secrets, sees in the dark – light spills out of him."*[13] Therefore you should be ready to accommodate changes as God directs you.

Application Suggestion

1) What steps will you take to ensure specificity and flexibility of your goals?
2) What milestones will you set to measure your accomplishments?
3) What critical timelines will you set to accomplish your goals?

Goal A:________________________________

Timeline:______________________________

Goal B:________________________________

Timeline:______________________________

Goal C: _______________________________

Timeline_______________________________

"Your goals must represent a vision towards which you have the willingness and ability to work"

ഇര

CHAPTER 8

Prioritizing Your Goals

"The key is not to prioritize what's on your schedule, but to schedule your priorities"

~ Stephen Covey ~

At one point or another, you have probably been overwhelmed by items on your so called 'to-do list'. We face this all the time as we try to juggle multiple tasks and finally end up either not accomplishing any one of them or spending a lot of time and resources on one task at the expense of the others. The dilemma we face in making a decision on what task to perform at any given time may sometimes come at a cost.

In Luke 9:59-62, we see Jesus talk of two men who had to juggle between attending to their personal assignments and following Him. Jesus asked one of the men to come and follow Him, and the man answered, *"certainly, but first excuse me for a couple of days, please. I have to make arrangements for my father's funeral." Jesus refused. "First things first. Your business is life, not death. And life is urgent: Announce God's kingdom!" Then another said, "I'm ready to follow you, Master, but first excuse me while I get things straightened out at home." Jesus said, "No procrastination. No backward looks. You can't put God's kingdom off till tomorrow. Seize the day."*[1]

This scripture reminds us to get our priorities straight. Jesus made it clear that we only have so much time in which to respond to His call and do our appointed purpose without procrastination. Similarly, it is important that you lay down strategies on how you plan to approach your goals.

As Eleanor Roosevelt put it "It takes as much energy to wish as it does to plan". Failure to plan is planning to fail. Plan to plan, and the Lord will always bless the work of your hands.

Now that you have set specific, measurable, attainable, realistic and time-bound goals (SMART goals); the next step is to prioritize these goals and tasks. I will walk you through a three-stage process that will help you accomplish this.

First Things First

Each one of us does prioritize in one way or another either intentionally or unintentionally as we attend to our daily chores. Paul's epistle to the Ephesians describes the sequence of putting on the full armor of God.[2] This is a good example of proper prioritization in a stepwise progression:

1. Stand firm
2. Buckle the belt of truth around the waist
3. Have the breastplate of righteousness in place
4. Fit the feet with the readiness
5. Additionally take up the shield of faith

Prior to implementing your vision, it is critical that you map out the entire vision by determining all that it will entail. This may include defining the processes you intend to use in executing the goals and gathering the needed resources. It also involves compartmentalizing your vision into goals and tasks that are specific, measurable, attainable, and that are realistic. You categorize your goals and tasks in the right order or hierarchy to ensure that they complement each other and are relevant to your vision.

Break down the entire vision into small manageable goals and tasks.

In this chapter we will discuss three unique stepwise approaches or stages that you can employ to prioritize your goals. This stepwise process will help you break down your vision into small manageable goals and tasks that can then be prioritized in terms of urgency, importance and relevance to your vision. These three distinct stages are:-

- Stage 1: The mapping stage using *the MAP approach.*
- Stage 2: The Positioning stage using *the GPS approach.*
- Stage 3: Task prioritization stage using *the Bull's eye task matrix.*

THE MAP APPROACH (MAPPING STAGE)

In the mapping stage you take a bird's-eye view and see the very broad and comprehensive picture of your vision using *the MAP approach.* Think of it as using a map in which you have a very broad picture of your landscape.

While using a map you first determine your starting point and end point which is your destination. This will include determining the routes, major and minor highways and landmarks that you expect to see as you travel towards your destination. You begin with the end in mind.

In this stage you map your vision by detailing and describing the strategic maneuvers that you will employ to achieve your entire vision. When you use *the MAP approach* you:-

- Clearly state your vision. Use the details of *the Habakkuk plan* you established in chapter two.
- List all the goals that will help you accomplish your vision. At this stage you list all goals regardless of when you intend to accomplish them. This should include information that you gathered on 'SMART' goals described in the previous chapter while incorporating your strengths and weaknesses as well as opportunities and threats.

THE GPS APPROACH (POSITIONING STAGE)

The GPS approach is literally taken from the GPS system of navigation and adopted as a goal-prioritizing concept. Effective use of the GPS navigation system requires that you determine only your starting and your end point. Unlike using a map, when you use the GPS system, details of each turn or maneuver are relayed to you just in time to use.

In this stage of planning, you break down your vision into major phases. You address your vision in stages, one phase at a time. You determine the fine details or the goals of the phase that you are working on at that given moment. This will keep you from being overwhelmed by the effort, time and resources needed to accomplish the entire vision. In this stage you:

- Break down the entire vision into phases. The number of phases will depend on the scope of your vision and the resources available.
- Assign the goals listed in the mapping stage to a given phase of your vision.
- Starting with the first phase, identify the long term goals. These will be the goals that you intend to achieve over a longer period of time, in most cases in more than a year.
- List the short term goals associated with the long term goals. These will be goals that you can realize in the near future probably within the

next few days, weeks or months.

- List all the tasks that will help you accomplish the goals associated with the first phase.
- Determine the resources needed to complete the goals and tasks in the first phase.

In this stage, you have to be keen and monitor the goals to ensure that they are always in alignment with your vision. This approach will help you avoid conflicting goals and will also improve allocation of available resources. Details for subsequent phases are defined just prior to the end of the current phase.

THE BULL'S EYE TASK MATRIX (TASK PRIORITIZATION STAGE)

Once you have broken down your vision into phases and have identified the goals and tasks for the first phase, the next step is to prioritize these tasks. It is important that you carefully evaluate the relevance of each task to your overall vision and establish a timeline for completion.

ജ്ജ

Prioritize tasks in terms of urgency, importance and relevance to your vision.

ജ്ജ

Prioritizing and establishing a timeline is the key that opens the door of action and closes the door of procrastination. If every task was a priority, there are higher chances that very little would be accomplished. Spending time on tasks that are not relevant to the accomplishment of your vision leads to a waste of precious time and resources.

The Bull's eye task matrix helps you prioritize the tasks

you identified in the positioning stage in order of their relevance, urgency and importance in relation to your vision.

The approach closely resembles the Eisenhower urgent/important matrix that was popularized by Dr. Stephen Covey as a time management tool in his book 'The Seven Habits of Highly Effective People'. However *the Bull's eye task Matrix* adds the concept of relevance of the tasks to your vision in order to clearly help you visualize how each task is pertinent to your vision. The matrix consists of five concentric zones each defining the level and relevance of each goal to your vision, which I refer to as *'the Bull's eye'* or *'the Nucleus'*.

In this stage, prioritize your tasks by first determining their urgency and importance and assign these tasks to a given zone. Then, in each zone rank the tasks by determining their level of relevance to your vision. Within a zone, assign the more relevant tasks closer to the base and the nucleus of the matrix. In each zone, tasks that are closer to the base should be addressed first because they are more relevant to your vision.

This stage helps you deal with the most urgent tasks, and those that are relevant to your vision while still not losing sight of the important tasks. The matrix is represented by:-

- The Nucleus / Bull's eye/ Vision
- Zone of Urgent and Important tasks
- Zone of Important but not Urgent tasks
- Zone of Urgent but not Important tasks
- The Crust/ The Peripheral (Zone of Not Urgent and Not Important tasks)

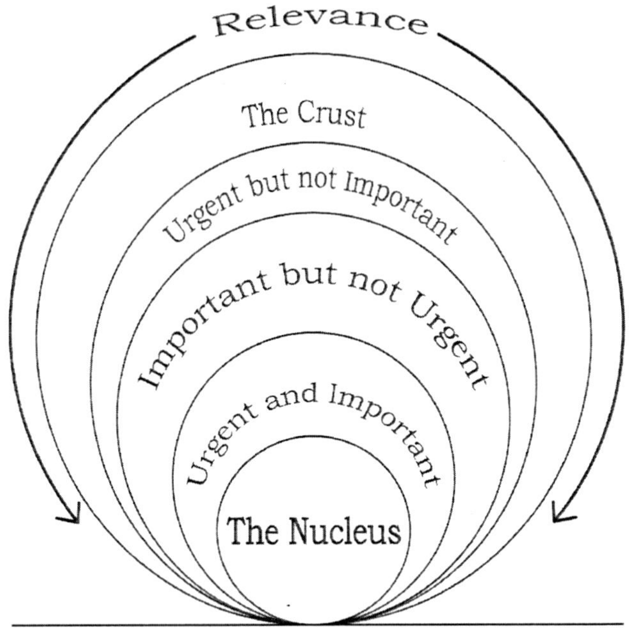

The Nucleus / Bull's eye/ Vision

The nucleus or the bull's eye is your vision as we described in chapter two. It is the core and the brain of what you want to achieve. All your goals and tasks should be prioritized around this zone.

The purpose of this zone is to ensure that you do not lose focus of your ultimate target. The relevance of your tasks should be determined by what level (zone) the task is located and how close in that level it is to your vision or the nucleus.

The Zone of Urgent and Important Tasks

The tasks that you list in this zone are the critical ones that need addressing immediately. These are the tasks that will make everything else come to a standstill if they are not dealt with immediately. They are both urgent and important to achieving your vision.

As Jesus and His disciples were crossing the Sea of Galilee, *"a fierce storm came up. High waves were breaking into the boat, and it began to fill with water. Jesus was sleeping at the back of the boat with his head on a cushion. The disciples woke him up, shouting, "Teacher, don't you care that we're going to drown?" When Jesus woke up, he rebuked the wind and said to the waves, "Silence! Be still!" Suddenly the wind stopped, and there was a great calm."*[3]

In this story, the rough winds made it difficult for the disciples to achieve their goal of sailing to the other side of the Sea of Galilee. The disciples wanted to address the most urgent and important issue immediately. They had no time to waste. They had to wake Jesus up and let Him calm the seas.

Plan appropriately to minimize urgent and important tasks, they represent crisis.

When you are faced with urgent and important tasks; determine how relevant they are to your vision before you address them. Take time and evaluate what resources you might have at hand to address the crisis. Some tasks in this zone may seem *'urgent and important'* to you but they are probably just *'important but not urgent'*.

When Martha was faced with Lazarus sickness, she saw the urgency and importance of his healing. She overlooked the resource (Jesus) that was available to meet the need. If she was aware of the resource available to her, she would not have considered Lazarus healing as urgent.

To minimize crisis, it is important to evaluate the resources available. Since tasks in this zone seek to deal with crisis, all efforts should be made to minimize them and address them early enough.

The Zone of Important but not Urgent Tasks

This zone includes tasks that are very important but not necessarily urgent. These tasks need not to be overlooked as they form a very fundamental part of achieving your goals. They are the preparation tasks that form the backbone of your strategy.

Tasks that you allocate to this zone have the potential to make a huge impact on you vision depending on how they are handled. Most of your tasks should fall in this zone. Plan to pay more attention to tasks in this zone. You may choose to use the 80/20 Pareto principle that we saw earlier to allocate ample time to work on these tasks without procrastination.

Review the importance and relevance of these tasks as they relate to your vision, that of your family, your ministry and also your circles of influence. Delaying these tasks may cause an inward shift to the next level of the inner zone where you will be required to address them with urgency and time may not allow. For example, developing a business plan is a very important task that should be addressed prior to starting a business. Failure to have a business plan may lead to crisis as you try to figure out the 'what', 'when' and 'how' of your business.

In Luke 10:38-42, we see the same experience with Mary and Martha as they received Jesus in their house.

Though Martha had welcomed the guests to their house, she had not made the necessary preparations for the visit which was an important task. As a result this turned into a crisis when the guests arrived.

We see Martha putting all her attention and efforts to preparations while Mary opted to be with Jesus their guest. If only Martha had prepared in advance, she would not have faced crisis trying to prepare while the guests were already in the house. The most important task at the time was to be with their guest.

In verses forty one and forty two we actually see Jesus underscore the importance of spending time with Him at that particular moment than being in the kitchen preparing for the guests.

It is therefore necessary to address the important tasks even though they are not urgent to prevent them from turning into an emergency. When we fail to address tasks that are important but not urgent, we will face challenges trying to addresses them when we have little or no time.

The Zone of Urgent and not Important Tasks

Tasks that fall in this zone are the ones that may interrupt you from achieving your vision. These tasks may interfere with your schedule and prevent you from completing your work.

In most cases these tasks are not on your 'to-do' list and usually results from pressure and demands from those around you when they fail to play by the 7 Ps (Proper Prior Planning and Preparation Prevents Poor Performance) rules that we saw earlier. These are the tasks that might be urgent to another party but not necessarily urgent or important to you.

Since you don't live in isolation, you need to help others when they are in need; however, that should not be interpreted to mean that others should poorly plan their activities and inconvenience you with their 'emergencies'.

Ask for God's wisdom to discern which of these tasks need your immediate attention. In most cases, these tasks should be rescheduled and addressed at your own convenience.

Occasionally, your may notice that some of the tasks initially assigned to this zone are actually relevant to your vision in which case they can be reassigned accordingly. Closely monitor these tasks and minimize or eliminate them from your to-do-list.

Pursuing the Crust is like chasing the wind.

The Crust (Zone of not Urgent and not Important Tasks)

The Crust consists of tasks that are neither urgent nor important to your vision. In this zone, you need to list tasks that are a distraction to your vision and those that are not worth your time.

These tasks should be avoided at all cost. Some tasks may seem necessary to work on but pursuing them is like *'chasing the wind'.*[4] Tasks that are not geared towards your vision should be assigned to the furthest part of the zone. However, over time some tasks in this zone may become more relevant to your vision in which they would be reassigned to the urgent but not important category.

This zone of tasks also serves as the 'parking lot' for tasks that you think may become relevant to your vision and that may be assigned to any other zone at a future date.

Once you've completed the first phase, repeat the prioritizing process for the remaining phases until you accomplish your vision.

Application suggestion

Short term and long term goals

1) What are your long term goals?
2) What short term goals are associated with the above long term goals?

The Bull's eye Task Matrix work sheet

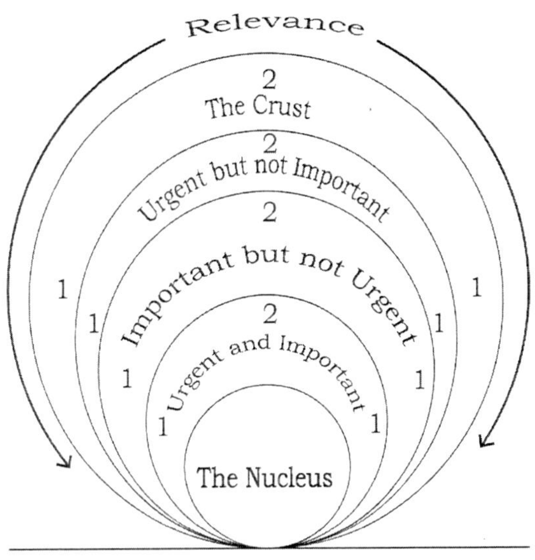

1) Use *the Bull's eye task matrix* above to prioritize the tasks associated with your first goal. Note: Task one (1) is more relevant to your vision than task number two (2).

Define your Nucleus / Bull's-eye/ Vision____________

List the urgent and important tasks

List the important but not urgent tasks

List the urgent and not important tasks

List the not urgent and not important tasks (The Crust/ The Peripheral)

"God made us in His own image and likeness, therefore just like Him, we have an inherent ability to plan unless we choose not to exercise that ability"

ജ്ഞ

CHAPTER 9

Implementing Your Goals

"Goals are dreams we convert to plans and take action to fulfill"

~ Zig Ziglar ~

Defining your vision and setting your goals are important steps towards your greatest success. However you can only reap the fruits of your vision when you implement those goals. Your action plan will be the cornerstone of effective goal execution.

Execute your Plan

As mentioned earlier, you need to implement your action plan for you to reap the full benefits of the planning strategy. It is not uncommon to find ourselves planning but fail to take that first step towards executing our plan.

Out of fear, we may start to give excuses as to why we are delaying the execution. Now that you have carefully prioritized your goals; take that first step and overcome the fear. Actually, the clarity of your vision comes when you face your fears head-on.

Do this by taking a proactive approach rather than waiting for what you may regard as the opportune time to act. Do not sit on that great vision that you have established.

Clarity of your vision comes when you face your fears head-on.

The impact of the dynamite power of an explosive can never be realized unless detonated. Likewise the horsepower of an engine may not be realized until you crank it. You have a great weapon; don't just let it sit in that depot, unleash the potential in you and you will see the full impact of what is within you.

Have a Sense of Urgency

Luke 9: 57-62 reads that no man putting his hand to the plough, and looking back, is fit for the kingdom of God. In the parable of the great banquet, when the invited guests failed to show-up, the master told his servants to "*Quickly, get out into the city streets and alleys. Collect all who look like they need a square meal, all the misfits and homeless and wretched you can lay your hands on, and bring them here."*[1] This shows the sense of urgency that the master had on the feast. It is a great teaching on how you need to approach your vision with urgency.

You probably have heard of a Chinese proverb that reads, "A journey of a thousand miles must begin with a single step." This means that in the process of achieving your great vision; you may start with those small steps. They are worth the shot than not taking any step at all.

These small steps are excellent start; however, use them as stepping stones and do not settle there. Aim to make that first giant leap of faith and soon you will find out that you can walk or run.

Do not procrastinate since this is the day that the Lord has made for your blessings to start flowing - procrastination is the thief of time. Delay only in instances of divine procrastination during which you are seeking God's direction for the next move.

Start working on your goals early enough by making the most of every opportunity and to avoid crunch time decisions that may not support the vision the Lord has given you. Make efforts to adhere to your timelines.

In most cases we procrastinate as a result of failure to stick to our targeted deadlines. By not starting on a specific project, you are forfeiting a lot for your future and that of your family.

Be Available to Champion your Dream

You may have the vision and all resources needed, but without your availability, your vision may just be a dream. When the Lord grants you a vision, be available to champion it.

Dr. Dot Richardson, the 1996 American Olympic team softball captain and a physician observed that a true champion is someone who wants to make a difference and a person who never gives up. A champion gives everything they have no matter what the circumstances are. A true champion works hard and never loses sight of their dreams.

You have to be available for God to use you and to work on the vision. The vision belongs to you and you do not expect other people to lead or take all the initiatives. If you are working with a team, it is your responsibility to re-energize your base. A champion will see a door of opportunity when others see a wall and no way out. As a champion you will derive energy from any resistance you face.

A champion sees a door where others see a wall.

Do not over delegate to a point where other people are actually running your vision while you are absent in all undertakings. Do not be an absent visionary. Those around you are there to help you accomplish the vision but they are not the vision carriers. Though you may not have the skills or the tools to achieve a given task, be available.

Give directions to those the Lord has brought to you to support your vision. *"The very moment you separate body and spirit, you end up with a corpse. Separate faith and works and you get the same thing: a corpse."*[2] Take a step and do what you need to do to achieve your vision. Stop making excuses, stop procrastinating and start working on the vision God has given you.

Be an Innovator

Innovation is a key component of any successfully implemented vision. It is the art of discovering the full potential of the rod in your hand and reinventing yourself accordingly. It is when you defy the popular approach of achieving an outcome and employ your creative ideas to achieve a popular outcome.

We need to continuously be creative and look for alternative methods of approaching our vision. Just because someone else successfully used a given technique to accomplish a goal doesn't necessarily mean that, that was the most innovative way of doing it. As Albert Szent-Gyorgyi put it "discovery consists of seeing what everybody has seen and thinking what nobody has thought".

Make all efforts to approach things differently. Luke 5:17-26 gives an account of a paralyzed man who was brought to Jesus to be healed. When the men that brought him saw that the house was crowded and that there was no room for them to get in; they removed the tiles from the rooftop and lowered the man right to where Jesus was.

These men were very innovative in their approach. They would have chosen either to give up or to request people for room to pass all the way to where Jesus was. Or perhaps they would have decided to wait and maybe catch-up with Jesus on his way out; but they opted to take a risk, be innovative and do what was outside the norm.

As you face familiar scenarios in your implementation process, apply unusual approaches and you will achieve unusual results.

Evaluate your Progress

Frequently evaluate and grade your work using a predetermined scale that you are comfortable with. Often people prefer to use a one to ten scale. The goal for this is not to see your failure rather to see if there is need for a change in strategy. It will also help you with future planning and allocation of resources. Evaluating your progress will make you appreciate what the Lord can do through you.

Do not be an absent visionary.

As we saw earlier in the story of creation, God concluded each stage by evaluating what He had created that day. At the end of each day, God marked the milestone by evaluating what He had made and concluding that it was good. On the sixth day after He had created everything, the scripture says that He saw all that He had made, the entire work of creation was very good.

God is omniscient, He is perfect and His ways are perfect, yet He looked back and evaluated His work of creation. Similarly you should honestly evaluate your work at all stages and upon completion to ensure that the work meets the desired outcome.

Regularly assess your vision to ensure that it is still God-centered and aligned with your spiritual values, family values, area of service and your professional and social circles that we saw in chapter three.

In case there is misalignment, refocus and get back on track. Realigning your vision early enough will require less effort to mend compared to the effort and resources required to restore a derailed vision that is no longer centered on God's will.

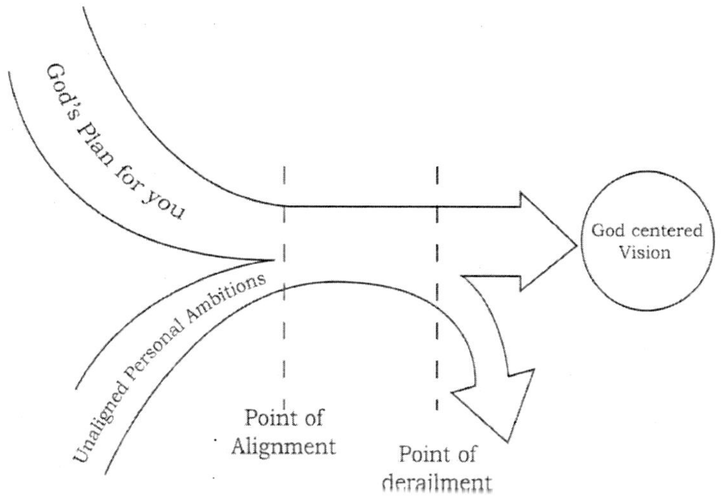

Watch out for some of the most common symptoms of a derailed vision which may include lack of desire to commit a vision to God in prayer, pride, ego, or the 'me' and 'I' syndrome especially on team assignment. In a derailed vision, the vision carrier wants their might and influence to be seen. Derailed visions may however seem to succeed but they do not bring glory to God but to man unless they are restored.

Some of the ways to assess if your vision is still in alignment is to seek God in prayers as we will see later. It is also possible to discover misalignment by listening to those within your inner circles as they will often be the first ones to notice.

Antagonism and conflict with your other areas of stewardship may also be a sign of misaligned vision. Choose not to ignore any of those warning signs as a derailed plan would be too costly to fix.

From Baby Steps to Strides

Now that you have taken these steps of executing your goals, keep moving forward. Do not remain stagnant. Move from one level to the other.

Have the urge to grow and you will overcome the fear that holds you back.

One of my favorite bible verses is 1 Peter 2:2 (AMP), *"Like newborn babies you should crave (thirst for, earnestly desire) the pure (unadulterated) spiritual milk, that by it you may be nurtured and grow unto [completed] salvation."* In other words do not remain where you started rather take the next step. Have that urge to grow and you will overcome the fear that holds you back from achieving the greatest level of success.

You may have been used to your current situation thinking it is normal to earn what you earn, work where you work and live where you live but God has a bigger plan for you. Ask Him for new and deeper revelations that will move your vision to the next level.

Application suggestion

1) What strategies have you put in place to ensure that you execute your vision?
2) How will you ensure that you are available for your vision?

Innovation is the art of discovering the full potential of the rod in your hand and reinventing yourself accordingly.

PART IV

Let Go and Let God

ഇന്ദ

CHAPTER 10

Persevering in Dark Times

"Never think that God's delays are God's denials. Hold on; hold fast; hold out. Patience is genius."

~ Georges-Louis Leclerc ~

Your vision may seem to be a mirage that can never be reached. The goal may not be very clear from a distance; but that is the time to be persistent and to put efforts into your vision despite any difficulties, failure, opposition or other odds you may encounter. The goal post may seem to move as you approach your victory, but that is not the time to give up, rather it is the time to ask God for renewed strength.

Regardless of the situation, press on to your destiny. As a river flows from an upland source down to its mouth, it encounters many obstacles, hills, mounds, valleys and vegetation. The river in its course may meander around; go through or erode these landforms and vegetation.

As you move towards your destiny, you will encounter many challenges; do not give up, rather choose either to persevere through the challenge or be innovative and devise a path around it. However always be in tune with the Holy Spirit and obey God's direction. This may be a change in your course or a new vision altogether.

Choose to persevere through the challenges or be innovative and devise a path around them.

As Thomas A. Edison observed, our greatest weakness lies in giving up. Take courage in all that you do and when you face challenges. When one door closes, another will open, for God has a purpose for everything that happens to us. The most certain way to succeed is always to try just one more time.

You may have reached the darkest point of your vision, or there may be a cloud over your vision, be patient because showers of blessings are imminent.

Perseverance is a very important virtue that all Christians should have in their daily walk with Christ. It is also one of the qualities that most successful people employ in achieving their goals and overcoming the obstacles they encounter. It is the determination you put in despite the challenges that you may face.

Proverbs 24:16 says that, those who trust in God may fall seven times, but they will get up again. But one disaster is enough to bring down the wicked. Perseverance is the effort you put to rise up the eighth time after seven falls.

Be steadfast when you face challenges. *"We can rejoice, too, when we run into problems and trials, for we know that they help us develop endurance. And endurance develops strength of character, and character strengthens our confident hope of salvation. And this hope will not lead to disappointment. For we know how dearly God loves us, because he has given us the Holy Spirit to fill our hearts with his love."*[1]

Perseverance in Spite of Circumstances

As you work on your vision, you are prone to face challenges, but it is how you tackle these obstacles that matters. Despite the challenges, believe that you have God- given strengths and as His child, you are very valuable and precious in His eyes.

Be patient, the showers of blessings are imminent.

Think of a quarter dollar coin or any other coin currency. It may go through challenges in the course of exchange in the market place, but despite the disfiguration or being worn out, it still retains the original monetary value. It still has the same value as a new coin from the central bank.

Likewise, when you face challenges, you do not lose the value and potential that God has put in you. You are as valuable just as that brand new coin is. Even though both the old disfigured coin and the new coin have the same monetary value attached to them, you can only realize their full potential when you use the coins in the market place. You can only realize the potential in you when you put it into use. Be steadfast. Know that your potential does not diminish when you face challenges.

We see Joseph facing challenges in his life, yet he remained steadfast and persevered regardless of the circumstances.[2] His brothers sold him to slavery out of jealousy and lied about it to their father. While in Egypt, Joseph was sent to prison after being framed by Potiphar's wife for rape.

While he was in prison, Joseph helped Pharaoh's butler interpret a dream with a promise to remember him and plead his case. However once he had secured his release and was restored to his rank, the cupbearer never honored the agreement he had with Joseph.

Joseph remained faithful and focused on the gift of dreaming and dream interpretation even when in prison. God continued to use this gift and at the end, Joseph became victorious and was blessed with leadership. God positioned him in a rank where he was able to help his family when the famine stroke.

Despite the difficulties and challenges that you may go through, God is positioning you for a blessing. Seize the moment and remain steadfast and faithful. Do not despise any opportunities or tasks that come your way or see them as too minor. Be faithful in those small tasks or opportunities because God can use them as a stepping stone to take you to the next level.

In jail, Joseph persevered and never despised the cupbearer and the baker. He remained faithful to his call and interpreted the dreams for them. If God could see the faithfulness in interpreting dreams for the fellow inmates, He could also entrust him with interpreting big dreams for the king.

If you can persevere and remain faithful with the small responsibilities that you've been entrusted; God will be faithful and will trust you with the ability to handle bigger responsibilities.

Perseverance in Roadblocks

Sometimes you may encounter challenges and roadblocks that lead to a failure or disappointing setback of your vision. Often, such failures may lead one to procrastinate or give-up the pursuit of their vision. In such situations, it is important to know that a bend on the road does not mean the end of the road.

Roadblocks may cause a delay on your timeline, but they should never stop you from achieving your vision.

Roadblocks are to be expected and as Thomas A. Edison, the inventor of the incandescent light bulbs said, just because something doesn't do what you planned it to do doesn't mean it's useless.

The scripture says that God will bless the works of our hands. This takes me back to the story of Nehemiah rebuilding the wall of Jerusalem. Despite opposition and ridicule from Sanballat, Tobiah and Geshem, Nehemiah persevered and pressed on with the project to completion.[3] Nehemiah's ultimate goal was deeply rooted in his heart and mind and he was not to waver despite the mockery.

When you face criticism, do not be distracted or feed

yourself with the negativity. Sometimes choosing to ignore negativity may be the best way to move on to your God - planned destiny. If you believe these negative comments, you will be feeding your heart with unbelief instead of faith.

A roadblock on the road may cause a delay but it does not stop you from reaching your destination, it is not a dead-end. In the same manner, roadblocks may cause a delay on your timeline, but they should never stop you from achieving your vision.

Perseverance When you Face the Unknown

As I mentioned earlier, your vision may seem to be a mirage and unclear. You may have just embarked in a new territory that still remains unclear to you. Do not give up; you are headed to a greater freedom than you have now. God may be preparing you for something beyond your imagination.

Think of the Pilgrims on their Mayflower voyage as they set from Europe to Plymouth. It was not clear to them where they were going or where they were to settle, but they never gave up. Their perseverance in search of religious freedom led to the birth of United States of America as we know it today.

I am also reminded of the German missionaries to Africa, Johann Ludwig Krapf and Johannes Rebmann. The two were among the first Europeans and missionaries to Africa in the mid 1800's. They faced challenges and hostile environments including diseases such as malaria; wild animals and travel challenges as they spread the gospel across North and East Africa.

During the course of their missionary work, they were mocked back in Europe and were reported to be suffering hallucination from malaria just because they reported to have seen snow on the cap of what is now Mt. Kenya and Mt. Kilimanjaro in East Africa.

Despite the challenges, the two remained steadfast in their determination to preach the gospel for over twenty five years. They opened up the Northern and Eastern Africa to other missionaries and explorers. Today most parts of Africa are deeply rooted in Christianity as a result of their work.

Always have the courage and perseverance as you face the unknown. Remain steadfast, immovable, and always abounding in the work of the Lord, knowing that in the Lord your labor is not in vain.[4] Remember this is not your working but the Lord working through you. You sought His counsel for a vision and He gave it to you, He will bless it as you persevere.

Perseverance When There Seems to be no Help

In the New Testament we read of the story of Jesus healing a paralytic by the pool who had been there for thirty eight years.[5] The scripture says that every time he tried to get into the pool, someone else got in first. He had no one to assist him but he never gave up. This applies to us as we press on with our goals.

Sometimes the conditions may not work in your favor or you may not have the 'right' connections. Take courage and press on, the right person or conditions will come your way when you least expect it. '*Jesus will come your way earlier than expected.'*

Just before the water is stirred up next time, you will have your breakthrough. May it be a promotion at work or a project that you are undertaking; do not rely on seasons, be persistent and have faith; you will soon see your breakthrough. The darkest hour comes just before the dawn. You may be the underdog, but soon you will be an overcomer.

As Jesus was teaching His disciples on persistence in prayers, He told them of the parable of the persistent widow.[6] The widow was persistent in asking for justice despite refusal by the unjust judge.

We see at the end the judge granted her justice because she kept on bothering him. Though the focus of this parable was to teach us to be persistent in prayers, the actions by this widow clearly show why we should never give up.

You may be the underdog but soon you will be an overcomer.

You have probably heard of the 212 degrees principle. If pure water at sea level was heated to 211 degrees Fahrenheit, it would be extremely hot but would not boil. However, by heating just one extra degree the water reaches the boiling point; boils and even changes from the liquid state to vapor state. It is this change of state that is so powerful even to move a steam engine.

When you are about to give up, it is this one degree (persistence) that you need to help you move to the next level. Keep on praying and ask God to give you strength to keep going. *"For everyone who asks and keeps on asking receives; and he who seeks and keeps on seeking finds; and to him who knocks and keeps on knocking, the door shall be opened."*[7]

Perseverance When the Vision Tarries

Sometimes you may face delay in accomplishing your vision. You may not know the cause of the delay, but God may be preparing you for the great responsibilities during the waiting period.

Probably you have wondered why it took Jesus thirty years before He started His ministry and three years in the actual ministry before He left to be with the Father. The initial thirty years were preparation years.

The story of Moses is another good example of the importance of perseverance when your vision tarries. As God prepared him to deliver the children of Israel, Moses lived among the Egyptians for forty years during which he saw their suffering in captivity and also learned the wisdom of the Egyptians.

He later spent another forty years in exile in Midian away from the Egyptians and the Israelites during which period he had an encounter with God. We later see him accomplishing God's purpose by spending forty years in the wilderness with the Israelites as they headed to Canaan after he helped them escape from slavery in Egypt.[8]

Moses may have been impatient wondering when he will ever accomplish his mission, but during his first eighty years, God was molding him for the task. Do not be impatient; a delay is not a denial.

Perseverance When you Face the Giants

Sometimes the challenges you face as you work on our goals

seem like giants that are hard if not impossible to overcome. You probably have heard of the story of a young Israelite shepherd boy named David and a Philistine's giant called Goliath.

The Philistine took advantage of the nine foot tall giant and fought the Israelites. They challenged the Israelites for a match up with the hope that no one would ever defeat the giant.

David, the unarmored boy responded to Goliath, *"you come to me with sword, spear, and javelin, but I come to you in the name of the LORD of Heaven's Armies – the God of the armies of Israel, whom you have defied."*[9] Using his sling, David knocked down and killed the giant.

In the same way, you may face challenges that seem too huge to overcome, gather courage and take the sling that the Lord has put on your hand.

Those around you may look and not see the rod or the sling that the Lord has put in your hand. They may look and see just a 'shepherd boy', but God sees a great and brave warrior and a king who overcomes.

Boldly face the giant in front of you and do not be intimidated by its size. See the big God in you and not the mountain, and as long as you have the conviction and strength of resolve on your side you will overcome.

When you face giants and mountains, just remember that it is not by your own might, nor by your power, but it is through the Spirit of God that you will overcome. God will level down any mountain that may seem to be too big to climb.[10] You are in the perfect will of God. Nothing happens by coincidence or chance.

Perseverance Even When you Fail

Sometimes you will fail, but as Joyce Meyer asserts in her book 'Any Minute', "One mistake does not have to rule a person's entire life." One failure should not stop you from pressing on; keep going, for in a race all runners run, but only one receives the prize, therefore run so that you may obtain it.[11]

Most of God's servants in the scripture went through challenges of one kind or the other but they never quit in their mission. Not even Peter gave up despite having denied Jesus three times. As Vince Lombardi once put it, "Winners never quit, and quitters never win." You may have missed the mark this time around, but keep going; you are in God's perfect will.

Marking time? You are about to receive your marching order.

Perhaps after putting a lot of effort, you found out that you have just been marking time; press on, you are about to receive your marching order.

You may be ambitious in trying to achieve your goals but it is your steadfastness that will keep you moving towards your goal. Many inventions that we see today were as a result of great perseverance on the part of the inventors. If God has called you and given you a vision, He has a purpose for it and he will bring it to completion.

Just like Abraham on Mt. Moriah, wait upon the Lord, there is a ram caught by its horns in a bush close to you.[12] It may be that God wants you to take a different direction or reinvent your approach.

Conditions may not look perfect or possible but the Lord is saying that He is *"doing a new thing! Now it springs forth; do you not perceive and know it and will you not give heed to it? I will even make a way in the wilderness and rivers in the desert."*[13]

Whenever you face challenges and everything seems to have come to an end, persevere and know that it is just a bend not the end, soon after you will see a new horizon.

Learn From Failures

Most people fear to fail. Failure makes us feel powerless. Do not let a past failures hold you back. Often, failure is the mother of all success; the only way to avoid failure is to fail to do anything in which case you've actually failed.

Failure by itself is not bad, what's bad is failure to learn from your failures. Thomas Edison, after more than 10,000 attempts to invent the incandescent light bulb, observed that, he had not failed but had just found 10,000 ways that didn't work.

Learn from the shortcomings but do not dwell on them. It may seem as if failures are slowing you down, but be optimistic and learn from them. Slowing down is not necessarily bad, it may be for your own good. When you see that 55 miles per hour sign on a freeway, the goal is not to delay you but it is to slow you down for your safety and those around you.

Throughout the scriptures we see characters that failed time and again yet the Lord continued to use them in great ways. King David, a man after God's heart failed numerous times, but David never ceased to serve God. He learned to rise-up, repent and move on every time he failed.[14]

By accepting to learn from your mistakes, you show willingness to be corrected and counseled.

Perseverance When the Enemy Comes Fighting

Sometimes you may get discouraged and see as if the enemy is attacking you from all fronts - take courage and persevere. God is going to use the same weapons that the enemy is using against you to promote you. God used the same fire the enemy wanted to use against Shadrack, Meshack and Abednigo, to kill the adversary.[15]

We see this also happen to Mordecai as he faced challenges and was almost hanged in the gallows that Haman had prepared. Mordecai continued to be faithful and to serve as a guard and never ran from challenges.

He found favor with the king and became a power in the palace and his reputation grew all over the land. On the other hand Haman was hanged on the same gallows he had planned to kill Mordecai.[16]

As long as you are in God's perfect will, do not abandon your responsibilities and tasks.

As long as you are in God's perfect will, do not abandon your responsibilities and tasks even as you face challenges unless the Lord instructs you otherwise. When you are faced with fierce challenges, stay put; God is working behind the scenes. Have faith and know that your breakthrough is just around the corner. God may be using these challenges as your stepping stone to the next level.

You've probably heard of a story told of a man whose small boat capsized in the deep seas. The man clung on a raft that drifted to a nearby small island. Once safely on the island, the man built a small shack which unfortunately caught fire the following day.

The man worried of what to do next; questioned God on why he had to face such challenges that even his last hope had gone up in smoke. Little was the man aware that God's plan was to use the smoke to send an SOS distress signal to a ship a few nautical miles away to come to his rescue.

When challenges come and the enemy comes roaring, God may be pointing you to a different direction or He may be preparing you for a rescue. Just listen to His voice.

As the saying goes, God can turn any of the mess you find yourself in, into a message, any of the tests you go through into a testimony, any trial into a triumph, any victim into a victor and any trouble into a double portion.

Perseverance When you are Being Refined

According to James 1:12; you are blessed when you remain steadfast under trial, for when you have stood the test you will receive the crown of life, which God has promised to those who love him. When you go through challenges, persevere, they may be meant to make you better.

The scripture says that when you go through challenges, you get refined like gold and at the end of it all; it is for our own good. The intensity of the heat subjected to gold determines its purity.

The challenges may be unbearable, but the more refined and prepared you will be. Think of the yeast used in bread. It has to be heated to get that tasty and large bread. The leavened bread is usually larger than the dough. Likewise, you may experience some heat as you undergo expansion to higher levels of blessings.

You may encounter some dark moments, but rise up and shine. Just because it is cloudy where you are and you don't see the sun shine, it doesn't mean that the sun is not shinning elsewhere, persevere. The clouds will roll and the darkness will fade away and soon the sun will shine over your vision.

When you face challenges as you implement your God-given vision, just realize that it is not your vision that is being challenged; but it is the dreamer who is being refined.

Application suggestion

1) What are some of the obstacles/ roadblocks that you are trusting God to see you through as you execute your vision?

ꕥ

Just like an old disfigured coin; when you face challenges, you do not lose the value and potential that God has put in you

ꕥ

ꕥ

CHAPTER 11

Ploughing Back

"The noblest thing a man can do is, just humbly to receive, and then go amongst others and give"

~ David Livingstone ~

You may have probably heard economists use the term "plough back" to mean that they are reinvesting the returns or profits back into the business instead of distributing it to the owners.

Just as investors plough back their profits, always purpose to be part of the community that you live in by always giving back. Remember that the ultimate goal is that the Lord may be glorified. The Lord will continue to bless you out of your giving.

According to 2 Corinthians 9:11; you will be made rich in every way so that you can be generous on every occasion, and your generosity will result in thanksgiving to God. As the Lord increases your storehouse, purpose to be a blessing to His Kingdom, to the needy and to the community. As Sir Winston Churchill once put it "We make a living by what we get, but we make a life by what we give."

Your giving is not only a responsibility, but will also inspire others. God gave His only begotten Son. He wants you to give what He has freely entrusted you with; He is not asking for what you do not have. He freely gave His Son for our salvation.

Plough Back to the Storehouse

There are several ways in which you can plough back into God's kingdom. The Lord commands us to bring ten percent of what we have and the first fruits back into the kingdom. This is a test of your obedience and it shows that you can be entrusted with what the Lord has given you.

Obeying this command is an indication that your vision is in alignment with God's word. Think of it as a promise to perform a given task or achieve a certain milestone to receive a reward in return.

When we pay our tithes, God promises to open the windows of heaven and pour out His blessings, that there will be no enough room to receive them. He is instructing us to bring our tithes so that there will be sufficient supplies in

His house. He is challenging us to test Him in this and see if He will not open up heaven and shower us with blessings beyond our imagination.

Abram praised God for what He had done and in return gave a tenth of everything.[1] Similarly Jacob set up a pillar as God's house and gave a tenth of all that was given to him.[2]

When you tithe, God has not only guaranteed to defend you against marauders and protect your belongings; but He also promises to bless your vine that it shall never fail to bear fruit for you in the field.[3]

God is committing Himself to deal with anything that destroys the fruits of your ground. This could be the fruit of your labor, your family, health, your business and all the projects that you embark on. The blessings of God will manifest and the nations will testify; "*and all nations shall call you happy and blessed, for you shall be a land of delight.*"[4]

You do not give out of abundance, but out of generosity.

However, when you fail to tithe, you walk under a financial curse. This means that regardless of your hard work and no matter how much you earn you will face challenges. The devourer is allowed into your life and may destroy your family, health, or finances. Therefore, be sure to set aside a tenth of all that your fields produce each year and take it to the house where you worship.

Giving an offering is a good gesture and whatever you decide to give should be of your own accord and not given reluctantly or under compulsion. The scriptures say that when you give, *"you will receive. Your gift will return to you in full – pressed down, shaken together to make room for more, running over, and poured into your lap. The amount you give will determine the amount you get back."*[5]

The hand that gives will be blessed and the blessing is directly proportional to the giving. If you give sparingly you will also reap sparingly and the same applies to the generous giver who will reap generously out of their generosity.

Plough Back to the Needy

Helping the needy is a good gesture since it also brings blessings into our life. The scriptures in Deuteronomy 15:10 talks about generosity in giving. It implores us to give generously to the needy and to do so without resentment in our heart. In return, you will receive a blessing in all your work and in everything you put your hand on.

Do not hold back blessing those in need.

Now that the Lord has blessed you in achieving your vision, do not forget and turn away from His promises, tap into these promises by helping others and your next project will be blessed. When it is within your reach, do not withhold blessing those in need.

Proverbs 28:27 declares a blessing to those who give to the poor for they will never want, but warns of a curse to those in a position to give but they do not.

Plough Back to the Community

Giving back to the community that you live in is not only a good thing to do, but it also brings "abundance of joy." You feel good about yourself when you help the community. Remember, you do not give out of abundance, but out of generosity.

Sometimes you may go through challenging times as did the church in Macedonia, but do not get weary of doing what is good. *"The trial exposed their true colors: They were incredibly happy, though desperately poor. The pressure triggered something totally unexpected: an outpouring of pure and generous gifts... They gave offerings of whatever they could – far more than they could afford! – pleading for the privilege of helping out in the relief of poor Christians."*[6]

There are many ways through which you can give back to the community. Your giving could be in form of resources or volunteering your time.

Giving back helps you create good relationship with those in your community and may open up some opportunities for you. It is also a good sign that you appreciate those who support you, whether directly or indirectly. It can be an opportunity for you to identify your strengths and weaknesses or even boost your self-esteem. It will help you gain and develop new skills that can become useful to you in future.

Let's say you volunteer as a bookkeeper or treasurer at your local church, school PTA or any other organization. You will learn skills that you can use for your personal finances or in your business. The interaction with others will boost your social connections and even open new opportunities for you to build your brand, reputation and public profile.

Over the years that I have been involved in community activities, I have not only discovered strengths that I never thought that I had, but it has helped me see things in a different perspective. I have taken it as a learning opportunity and also as an opportunity to share what the Lord has given me freely.

God always has a purpose for any interaction that you have with someone. Always seize the moment and make the most of every opportunity.

Helping in the community means that you are helping others achieve their visions. In doing so, they may in turn be a blessing to your vision.

For example, we see Joseph after being put in prison not only helping Pharaoh interpret his dreams but he also proposes to him some approaches to solve the problems in the dream he had interpreted. Pharaoh in return crowns him as a ruler.

King David in 2 Samuel looked back to his humble beginning and fulfilled the promise he had made to Jonathan who had helped him rise to power. He in return blessed Jonathan's son, Mephibosheth.

"Since you excel in so many ways – in your faith, your gifted speakers, your knowledge, your enthusiasm, and your love from us – ... excel also in this gracious act of giving."[7]

Plough Back to your Vision

Re-investing into your vision is an important aspect of growth and continuity of your vision. Aim for higher heights by reinvesting your resources, time and training into your vision. Have that zeal to expand and grow your vision.

In the book of 2 Timothy 2:2 we see Apostles Paul's desire to grow the ministry of God as he trained Timothy and others on the word and how to spread the gospel. *"You have heard me teach things that have been confirmed by many reliable witnesses. Now teach these truths to other trustworthy people who will be able to pass them on to others."*[8]

Plan to be life-long learner by improving your skills and also invest on training those who support you in your vision. This will ensure that your vision is continuously growing and expanding. Identify and train a few trusted individuals who can support and stand in the gap in your absence. This is not only a good succession plan to ensure that your vision does not stall in your absence; but also an opportunity for you to learn new skills.

Reinvest your monetary and non-monetary resources such as time into your vision as a way to grow and expand it.

Be a Faithful Steward

As you continue to increase in the Lord's blessings, take heed and be a good steward of the resources that the Lord has provided. Do not misuse the blessings that you just received; the blessings that you've spent sleepless nights petitioning the Lord; rather take care of these and even use them to bless others.

Misuse of these resources is a recipe for a vision in demise. The blessings of your God-centered vision may be as sweet as a teaspoon of honey but would be as sour as vinegar if ill-managed.

In Matthew 14:13-21 we see Jesus feeding about five thousand men with five loaves and two fish. There were twelve basketfuls of broken pieces of left overs picked up by the disciples. Despite the fact that He was a miracle working God with the ability make more bread and fish on demand; Jesus opted to be a good steward of the fruits of His miracle and directed the disciples to pick up the left overs.

As you start to reap the fruits of your vision, be accountable of those resources and do not be wasteful - you may not see another miracle come your way. After all, as the saying goes; 'fortune knocks but once at every man's door', this might be the only time that it knocks on your door.

In the same token, do not underutilize the resources that you've received from God. Make maximum use of them and you will receive an extra reward. Jesus in the parable of the three servants, gave an account of how the servants used the talents that their master had given them.[9]

When the master left for a journey he gave his servants some talents. Two of the servants took their talents and ploughed them back for returns. One of the servants decided to hide his talent and he never made use of it.

When the master returned from the journey, he was excited that the two servants had been good stewards of what they were given, and He blessed them with more. On the other hand the one servant that never ploughed back and failed to be a good steward received no reward and his talent was taken away from him.

Just as was the case with the two servants, purpose to be a good steward of the blessings you receive from your vision and the Lord, your Master will add more into your basket.

Maintain your Integrity

With success, comes the temptation to compromise our values and take short-cuts. We find ourselves wanting to achieve more and more and in the end we compromise and wreck our integrity.

Evaluate your vision regularly to ensure that it is in alignment with God's will. It is important to remember that your blessings are directly tied to your faithfulness and integrity. It is God's intention that we should always be faithful in what we do and be people of integrity.

He instructed Solomon to be faithful and walk with integrity. *"As for you, if you will follow me with integrity and godliness, as David your father did, obeying all my commands, decrees, and regulations, then I will establish the throne of your dynasty over Israel forever."*[10]

Never compromise or look for an 'easy way out'

Remain a person of integrity. Never compromise or look for the 'easy way out'. Instead be a magnet that attracts others to come to you with ideas, visions and dreams. With this the Lord will see your faithfulness and will reward you in return. He will continue to entrust you with more.

Leave a Legacy

As you work on your vision, purpose to leave a legacy. Let it be your desire to leave a mark that will be enjoyed by generations to come. The scripture tells us that *"a good and honest life is a blessed memorial; a wicked life leaves a rotten stench."*[11]

Choose to leave a memorial that will be a blessing and be told to future generations. Leave a legacy that will be an account of glorious acts that you did through Christ.

Let your actions be a testimony to the future generations. Have the desire to be more like Jesus Christ; who after His earthly ministry left an enduring legacy that has been passed from one generation to another.

It is never too late to have a legacy; this is the best way that you can plough back to the future generations.

Application suggestion

1) What areas have you identified that you can plough back your blessings?

The blessings of your God-centered vision may be as sweet as a teaspoon of honey but would be as sour as vinegar if ill-managed.

ജ്ഞ

CHAPTER 12

Sealing the Deal

"Don't pray when you feel like it. Have an appointment with the Lord and keep it. A man is powerful on his knees"

~ Corrie ten Boom ~

I do not mean to disparage prayers by having this as the last chapter in this book but over the years, I have realized that prayers seal the deal. It is from your knees that new revelations will be borne in your mind.

You've probably seen those automatic doors at your shopping mall with infrared detectors or motion detectors. When activated, as you approach the entrance, doors open automatically. In the same manner, when you activate your prayers, every time you seek God's guidance, doors will open one after the other as you walk to your destiny.

Be in tune with God and commit yourself to prayer. When I first mentioned about this book project to my pastor, he first paused and commented *"pray, I don't mean a ten-hour prayer; I mean ten minutes. You will get new revelations every time you go on your knees."*

You probably know that most corporate deals are not sealed in the boardrooms, but during hobnob at that corner coffee shop.

In the same way, the Lord wants you to come to Him that you may reason together. He is a mighty counselor and will give you fresh counsel every time you seek His face. Pray for his provision in all aspects of your vision and he will be faithful to see you through.

Pray for Wisdom and Knowledge

As you embark on your vision, ask God for knowledge and wisdom. The scriptures say that He gives wisdom to everyone in abundance and with no partiality or hypocrisy. That means whoever asks for wisdom will get it.

King Solomon asked God to give him an understanding so as to make good judgment and to discern what is good and evil. He humbly asked God for wisdom as he ruled over God's people. King Solomon was not selfish; he understood that the responsibility he had was to be a steward over God's people. This was not 'his plan' but God's plan.

As you pray, ask God for knowledge and wisdom on how to approach the entire project. Acknowledge that this is His plan over your life and let Him carry the burden for you. Pray for wisdom and knowledge among those that will be involved in accomplishing your vision.

As a result of your unselfish prayer, God will not only give you the wisdom and knowledge to work through your vision, but also riches and honor so that there shall not be anyone else like you.[1] Through your prayers He will deliver into your hands the wisdom of the wise and the knowledge of the ledger.

Pray for Direction and New Insights

> ഇഗ
> *I was once blind, but now I see'.*
> ഇഗ

Working on a new vision more often than not means having a paradigm shift in the way you see things or approach a task. It means learning to cast your net on the other side of the boat when you are used to the opposite side. It means fishing in broad daylight while everyone else is fishing when it is still dark.

For the outcome of your vision to be above the ordinary, you need extraordinary revelations. You will need to humble yourself and let the Lord instruct you and teach you in the way you should go; He will counsel you when His eye is upon you.[2] You might have already committed the entire vision to him, do not cease, for every time you go on your knees, you will tap new revelations.

Though Jesus had spit and put his hands on the eyes of the blind man from the village of Bethsaida, the man still had no clear sight of things.[3] He saw people as trees. It was after the second touch that he saw everything clearly.

The Lord will give you that second touch and new revelations. You will no longer see people as trees walking around, your sight and insights will be restored and you will see everything clearly. Your vision will have clarity. The Lord will help you to reinvent yourself and take on new directions. Out of new insights, you will confess that 'I was once blind, but now I see'.

As a result of prayers, you will do what seems not to be possible to man. The Lord has granted you the vision, ask Him to direct you and let His will be done.

Give Thanks

Perhaps one of the most common things that successful people fail to honor is to offer a prayer of thanks-giving. This is a prayer of appreciation for what the Lord has done. Through this prayer, you acknowledge that it is not through your strength that you have accomplished your vision, but it is God who has enabled you. You acknowledge that the vision is to bring glory to Him and not for your own pride.

I like the quote by one of my favorite authors, Brian Tracy: "Develop an attitude of gratitude, and give thanks for everything that happens to you, knowing that every step forward is a step toward achieving something bigger and better than your current situation."

One of the most important things you can do as you work on your vision is to pray every day and to give thanks for the far that God has brought you. Samuel marked the victory over the Philistine by setting up a huge stone between the cities of Mizpah and Shen and named it Ebenezer meaning *"up to this point the Lord has helped us!"*[4]

The Lord is pleading with us not to be worried about anything that we are working on but instead, we approach His throne with prayer and with thanksgiving. He wants us to be grateful. Meister Eckhart observed that "if the only prayer you said in your whole life was, "thank you," that would suffice".

During the entire process, give thanks but know there is still more to be done. Once Nehemiah completed the rebuilding Jerusalem's walls, he paused and observed the victory. However, he knew there was more work to be done. He had to start rebuilding people's hearts starting with those that opposed him.[5]

Application suggestion

With the understanding that each goal comes with a different need; and with a pledge to always commit my plans to the Lord; here is my daily humble prayer that will guide me through this vision.

A prayer honestly said will seal the deal.

ജ്ജ

My Final Thought

"Tell me about pride and greed, and I will show you the predators of a well-established, God- centered vision"

~ Peter Karanja ~

Now that you have read *REVEALED: PATHWAY to GREATNESS;* please allow me to share my final thoughts on the eleven revelations outlined in this book.

It is my prayer that as you work on your vision, you will let the Lord to remain the center piece of your endeavor. In all your endeavors ensure that He is glorified in your success. As I mentioned above, do not let greed, pride and immorality consume your hard-fought, well established God-centered vision.

You don't need to have lived outside planet earth to see very well established visions dissipate as a result of these predators.

My heart bleeds and aches to see these bring down well-known and less-known individuals; large and small churches and ministries; big and small corporations; nations and governments. These predators have no preference of an ecosystem from which they operate. From Africa to Asia; Australia to The Americas not to forget Europe, all are havens.

It is my prayers that your vision will be well aligned with all other responsibilities that you engage in. Ensure that you will not be guided by greed and ruled by pride at the expense of others.

As I mentioned elsewhere in the book, though teaspoon of honey is sweet for your cup of coffee; it will instantly dissolve in the high seas and will not be of any use. Do not ever forget your humble beginning lest you lose your taste.

As the psalmist said *"a single day in your courts is better than a thousand anywhere else! I would rather be a gatekeeper in the house of my God than live the good life in the homes of the wicked."*[1]

My final prayer is that the Lord will see you through your vision, that the Lord will bless you, the Lord will increase you and that you will never leave His dwelling. Amen!

Notes

Chapter 1

1. Ecclesiastes 2:11(NLT)

Chapter 2

1. 1 Corinthians 12: 11
2. Ecclesiastes 11:5 (NLT)
3. Psalm 40:1
4. 2 Peter 3:15-16
5. Acts 22:3
6. Proverbs 29:18
7. Habakkuk 2:2 (THE MESSAGE)
8. Genesis 37: 5
9. 2 Timothy 4: 14-15 (AMP)
10. Proverbs 18:15 (NLT)
11. Hosea 4:6

Chapter 3

1. Genesis 39, 40 and 41
2. John 1:35 – 43
3. Proverbs 13:20

Chapter 4

1. James1:6-8
2. Proverbs 3:5-6 (AMP)
3. Hebrews 11:11-12
4. Exodus 23:29-30 (NLT)
5. Philippians 4:8 (AMP)
6. Romans 12:2
7. 1 Chronicles 11:22-23
8. 2 Samuel 23:8-17
9. 1 Chronicles 11:11
10. Deuteronomy 31:6 (THE MESSAGE)
11. Deuteronomy 20:1, (THE MESSAGE)
12. Matthew 27:51 (AMP)
13. Esther 4:13-14 (THE MESSAGE)
14. Matthew 14:22-33

Chapter 5

1. Luke 14:28 (NLT)
2. Exodus 4:2-3; 14:16 (THE MESSAGE)
3. Exodus 4
4. 1 Timothy 4:14 (AMP)
5. Proverbs 1:5 (AMP)
6. Genesis 41:39-40 (AMP)
7. Ecclesiastes 11:6

Chapter 6

1. Luke 14:28-32
2. 2 Corinthians 12:9-10 (THE MESSAGE)
3. Proverbs 27:17 (AMP)
4. Ecclesiastes 10:10
5. Isaiah 54:17 (NLT)

Chapter 7

1. Proverbs 3:6
2. Psalms 37:23
3. Genesis 11:4, 9 (NLT)
4. Jeremiah 29:11 (NLT)
5. Nehemiah 2:11-18
6. Philippians 4:6
7. 1 Samuel 1:9-28
8. Isaiah 38
9. Ecclesiastes 7:18 (THE MESSAGE)
10. Proverbs 23:4 (NLT)
11. James 4:15 (AMP)
12. Matthew 1:1-17
13. Daniel 2:21 (THE MESSAGE)

Chapter 8

1. Luke 9:59-62 (THE MESSAGE)
2. Ephesians 6:13-16

3. Mark 4:37-39 (NLT)
4. Ecclesiastes 1:17 (NLT)

Chapter 9

1. Luke 14:21 (THE MESSAGE)
2. James 2:26 (THE MESSAGE)

Chapter 10

1. Romans 5:3-5 (NLT)
2. Genesis 37,39, 40, 41, 42
3. Nehemiah 6
4. 1 Corinthians 15:58
5. John 5: 1-15
6. Luke 18:1-8
7. Luke 11: 10 (AMP)
8. Acts 7:20-51
9. 1 Samuel 17:45
10. Zechariah 4: 6-7
11. 1 Corinthians 9:24
12. Genesis 22:1-19
13. Isaiah 43:19 (AMP)
14. Psalm 51
15. Daniel 3: 10- 30
16. Esther 7

Chapter 11

1. Genesis 14:20
2. Genesis 28:22
3. Malachi 3:11
4. Malachi 3:12 (AMP)
5. Luke 6:38 (NLT)
6. 2 Corinthians 8:2 (THE MESSAGE)
7. 2 Corinthians 8:7 (NLT)
8. 2 Timothy 2:2 (NLT)
9. Matthew 25:14-30
10. 1 Kings 9:4-5 (NLT)
11. Proverbs 10:7 (THE MESSAGE)

Chapter 12

1. 1King 3:13
2. Psalm 32:8
3. Mark 8: 23- 25
4. 1 Samuel 7:12 (NLT)
5. Nehemiah. 6:14-16

My Final Thought

1. Psalm 84:10, NLT

BIBLIOGRAPHY

Covey, Stephen R. *The 7 Habits of Highly Effective People: Powerful Lessons in Personal Change.* New York: Free Press, 2004.

Heath, Chip and Heath, Dan. *Made to Stick: Why Some Ideas Survive and Others Die.* New York: Random House, 2007.

Lieder, Yaakov. "*Inspiration and Entertainment: Goal Setting Joseph's Way.*" n.d. *www.chabad.org.* 19 December 2012.

Meyer, Joyce and Bedford, Deborah. *Any Minute.* New York: Faith Words, 2009.

Nationmedia. "*Cradle of education with little to show for it.*" n.d. *http://www.nation.co.ke.* 23 February 2011.

Nuber, Kevin. "*Personal Growth: Setting Christ-Centered Goals.*" 15 January 2013. *http://www.cbn.com* 19 December 2012.

Tracy, Brian. *Eat That Frog: 21 great Ways to Stop Procrastinating and Get More Done in Less Time.* San Francisco: Berrett-Koehler Publishers, 2007

Contact the author

http://www.booksbypeter.com
author@booksbypeter.com